The Cornish in Australia

The CORNISH in Australia

Jim Faull

J Faull

Australian Ethnic Heritage Series
General editor: Michael Cigler

AE Press
Melbourne, 1983

Australasian Educa Press Pty Ltd
(Incorporated in Victoria)
30 Mt Dandenong Road, Croydon, 3136
Tel. (03) 725 6955

First published 1983

THE CORNISH IN AUSTRALIA
is a volume in the
Australian Ethnic Heritage Series
General Editor: Michael Cigler, Melbourne.

National Library of Australia
Cataloguing-in-publication-entry
Faull, J.F. (James F.).
The Cornish in Australia
ISBN 0 86787 200 4

1. Cornish — Australia — History.
I. Title. (Series: Australian ethnic heritage series).

994'.0049167

Design by Derrick I. Stone Design
Typeset by ABB Typesetting, Collingwood, Victoria
Printed by Dominion Press Hedges & Bell, Victoria, Australia.

Contents

Foreword

The Australian Ethnic Heritage Series is finally a reality. *The Cornish in Australia* is the first book in this series. Like the other volumes which are to follow, it is about the people who helped to build Australia. Since the beginning of white settlement people of many different ethnic backgrounds have come to Australia from all corners of the world. But their participation in the development of their adopted land, their economic and cultural contributions, have not received the deserved exposure in accounts of Australian history.

The aim of this series is therefore to show that people of many cultures have left a permanent mark on Australia. Each group brought their skills and ideas, qualities and cultural traditions which have gradually become part of today's Australia.

It is envisaged that the ethnic heritage series will encourage Australians to be proud of their cultural roots. To others, this series offers new information about this long-neglected part of Australia's heritage.

Michael Cigler
General Editor

Sources and Acknowledgments

Two main sources were used for general details about the Cornish; my own book, *Cornish Heritage — A Miner's Story*, and Philip Payton's doctoral thesis, The Cornish in South Australia. Philip Payton's book, *Pictorial History of Australia's Little Cornwall*, and Oswald Pryor's book, *Australia's Little Cornwall*, were also very helpful.

Newspapers consulted were: *Yorke's Peninsula Advertiser, The Peak Downs Telegram, People's Weekly, The Register, South Australian News, Kadina and Wallaroo Times, The Australian Christian Commonwealth, Yorke's Peninsula Country Times, South Australian Gazette and Colonial Register.* Other books, pamphlets and articles used included: H. Alvey, *Burra: Its Mines and Methodism*; J. Arbery, *Trevena Family History*; I. Auhl, *Burra and District: A Pictorial Memoir*; I. Auhl, *Burra Sketchbook*; I. Auhl, *From Settlement to City: A History of the District of Tea Tree Gully 1836–1876*; J.B. Austin, *The Mines of South Australia*; Serle (ed.), *Australian Dictionary of Biography*; R.M. Barton, *Life in Cornwall in the Early Nineteenth Century*; G. Blainey, *The Rush that Never Ended*; W.L. Blamires and J.B. Smith, *The Early Story of the Wesleyan Methodist Church in Victoria*; I.C. Benson (ed.), *A Century of Victorian Methodism*; *Records of the Castlemaine Pioneers*; Helen Campbell, *Bendigo Gold — The Cornish People*; R. Charlton, *The History of Kapunda*; E.H. Coombe, *History of Gawler 1837–1908*; F. Cusack, *Bendigo; A History*; Ross Duncan, 'Case Studies in Emigration', *Economic History Review*, Vol. 16, 1963; *Dunstan Family History*; F. Dutton, *South Australia and Its Mines*; U.R. Emanuel, 'The History and Decline of the Mining Village Byng', *Australian Geographer* 1929; J. Flett, *The History of Gold Discovery in Victoria*; W.R. Glasson, 'Early Western Glimpses', *Journal of the Australian Methodist Historical Society* 1945; B. Kennedy, *Silver, Sin and Sixpenny Ale: A Social History of Broken Hill*; W.B. Kimberley, *Ballarat and*

District; W.B. Kimberley, *Bendigo and District*; A.R. Mills, *Kungna Tuko — A History of Kanmantoo*; W.F. Morrison, *The Aldine History of South Australia*; J.J. Pascoe, *History of Adelaide and Vicinity*; R. Paull, *Old Walhalla*; O. Pryor, *Cornish Pasty: A Selection of Cartoons*; M. Royal, *Perry's Past*; G. Serle, *The Golden Age*; K. Thomson and G. Serle, *A Biographical Register of the Victorian Parliament 1859–1900*; R. Wells, 'Early Mining in the Glen Osmond Area', *Tradition*, 1980.

The South Australian College of Advanced Education provided research funds which allowed me to search for traces of the Cornish in old mining areas of Victoria, New South Wales and Queensland. Roslyn Paterson assisted with research on Western Australia, Kevin Harris drew the maps, Stephen Yarrow developed the photographs and Roslyn Pledge typed the manuscript.

Thanks are due to the following for photographs: Ian Auhl (pp. 69); the South Australian Archives (pp. 5, 10, 13, 43, 47, 65, 71); the Premier's Department of South Australia (pp. 6, 113) and the National Trust of Victoria (p. 58, from "Historic Places of Australia, Volume 1"). The cartoon on p. 73 is from Oswald Pryor: *Cornish Pasty* (Rigby Publishers). I have been unable to trace a copyright holder for three illustrations (pp. 10, 45, 51).

1 The Homeland and Cornish Ethnicity

The study of ethnic groups in Australia has become a popular pastime in the last thirty years because of the growing awareness of multi-culturalism in our society. There is an obvious link between this growing awareness and the steady stream of migration into Australia since the second World War. But it should not be forgotten that Australia has always been a multi-cultural society and that ethnic groups have existed in the country ever since the First Fleet arrived in 1788. Those first arrivals, and others who soon followed, included Irish, Welsh and Scots in addition to English people and other nationalities.

The periodic Australian census details give some indications of ethnic groups in our society. Thus in 1891 New South Wales had a population which included 26.3 per cent Irish-born, Victoria had 15.7 per cent of its people born in Scotland, and Queensland and South Australia each had 9 per cent of its settlers who had been born in Germany.

All of the colonies showed, in 1891, that more than 40 per cent of their overseas-born were English. Contained within this figure there were groups of people who identified themselves as Cornish. Because of a distinctive background these people did not easily accept the label English but, despite this, because they came from Cornwall, which is an English county, census-takers placed them in one convenient category along with people from the thirty-eight other counties.

Cornwall is the extreme south-western county of England and it juts, finger-like, into the Atlantic Ocean. Its eastern border is marked mostly by the River Tamar and beyond that is Devon. From the Tamar to Land's End the surface of Cornwall is very irregular with collections of rugged hills alternating with stretches of moorland. Brown Willy (417 metres) is the highest point in the county. The coastline is famed for its wild, rocky scenery: along the north-western coast the long Atlantic breakers pound ceaselessly against rocky cliffs or else roll on to beaches that provide the best surf riding in England. Features such as this, plus many quiet coves along the southern coast, make Cornwall one of England's most favoured tourist areas. Tourism is also assisted by a climate which is the mildest in all England.

Cornwall's mild climate is also good for agriculture. Market gardeners near the southern towns of Penzance and Falmouth grow early flowers, fruit and vegetables for the London market. There are many good fields of oats and barley and the grasses of the moorlands support many sheep and cattle.

Fishing has always been important in Cornwall and pilchards, skate, mackerel and plaice are still landed at fishing ports such as Falmouth, Mevagissey, Looe, Fowey, Newlyn and St Ives.

At one time Cornwall supplied half of the world's copper and all of the United Kingdom's tin. Copper is no longer mined but tin mining, after virtually disappearing early in the twentieth century because of competition from cheap Malayan sources, has had a small revival in the last twenty years. There are now four tin mines that supply nearly a quarter of the domestic requirements for the whole country.

Camborne and Redruth, formerly two busy mining towns, are today the centres for engineering works, and some shipbuilding is carried out at Falmouth. St Austell is famous for its white clay deposits which are excavated in huge pits. The clay is the main ingredient of much of the pottery that is made further north in Staffordshire. Delabole, near the north coast, has a very old and well-known slate quarry, and granite is also quarried throughout the county.

Thus ordinary Cornish working people have been predominantly fisher folk, farmers and agricultural labourers, and miners: unlike other areas of England, the county has had no large concentration of urban unskilled labourers. This helps to explain the background of Cornish emigrants to Australia.

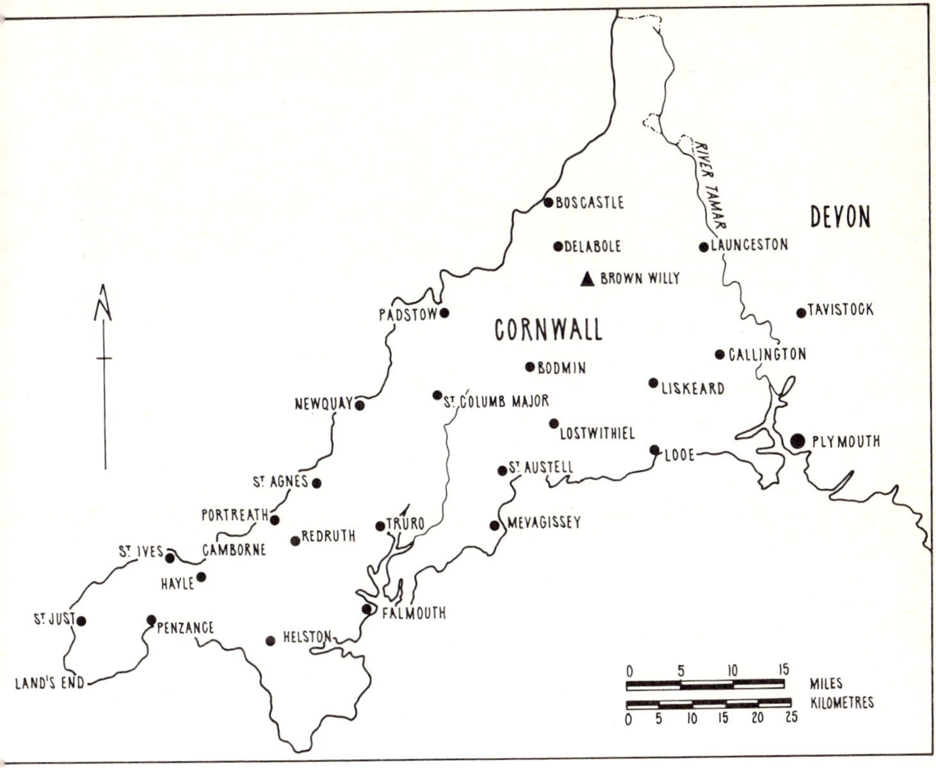

Map of Cornwall. The distance from Land's End to the River Tamar is slightly less than the distance from Melbourne to Bendigo.

People of true Cornish descent have always regarded themselves as ethnically different from the English. This is because of their Celt ancestry which stems from immigrants who came across the English Channel about 500 B.C. These Celtic-speaking people brought the Iron Age to Britain.

When the Romans and later the Anglo-Saxons invaded and conquered Britain, the original Celts were pushed westwards into Wales and Cornwall. The Cornish, or the West Welsh as they were sometimes called, stood apart from the rest of England until the ninth century before they were finally forced to acknowledge Anglo-Saxon supremacy. Today they still cling to many of their Celtic traditions and a Cornish-Celtic language was spoken right up until late in the eighteenth century. It was mixed with Anglo-Saxon terms but many distinctive words and names have continued to this day. Thus many Cornish surnames have the prefixes 'Tre', 'Pol' and 'Pen' which meant a dwelling, a pool and a headland or summit respectively. These prefixes are included in a well-known saying, viz:

By Ros, Car, Lan, Tre, Pol and Pen
Ye may know most Cornishmen.

Although the Cornish language was no longer used in the nineteenth century when many Cornish people were coming to Australia, the many unusual Celtic words, and a very distinctive brogue, made the speech of Cornish people different from that of their counterparts from the other counties of England. This was one of the most obvious indicators of ethnicity with the Cornish. Very often the adult immigrants kept their distinctive speaking habits until they died. Their children, however, quickly learnt a typical Australian way of speaking.

Cornishmen retained for a very long time a special feeling of separate identity. To them 'up-country' across the Tamar was a journey into England, virtually a foreign land. Their separateness manifested itself for example in their own song 'Trelawney' or 'The Song of the Western Men' which proudly proclaims in its stirring lines:

A good strong sword and a trusty hand,
  A merry heart and true,
King James's men shall understand what
  Cornish lads can do,
And have they fixed the where and when,
  And shall Trelawney die?
Here's twenty thousand Cornish men
  Will know the reason why!

If this song is the equivalent of a Cornish national anthem, then St Piran's cross is the equivalent of a national flag. A white cross on a black background, it commemorates one of the many Celtic saints who came to Cornwall preaching Christianity in the fifth and sixth centuries.

Yet another symbol of Cornish separateness is the tradition of the ruling monarch proclaiming his eldest son Duke of Cornwall; this gives the county a special link with the throne. Some true Cornishmen even use the tradition to recognise their land solely as a Duchy and not therefore merely as another English county. When a Duke of Cornwall was captured by the Saracens during the Crusades his release was obtained for the sum of fifteen gold coins. This was raised by voluntary subscriptions throughout Cornwall and the event is commemorated on the coat of arms for Cornwall which consists of fifteen gold balls and the motto 'One and All'.

The Cornish coat of arms, fifteen gold balls on a shield and the motto 'One and All'.

One notable feature of Cornish ethnicity was that a very large number of the people were devout Methodists. Nowhere was this more evident than in the Cornish miners who are discussed in Chapter 3. They had an outgoing approach to religion; singing was very much a part of their worship, and at the same time their entertainment. Carol singing, hymn singing and brass band music were part of the heritage that thousands took with them when they emigrated to Australia.

Entertainment for the Cornish in the nineteenth century featured a large number of fairs which took place on fixed days in the calendar. The fairs brought together a cross-section of the lower classes, not only the miners but also large numbers of poor fishermen and agricultural labourers. They mingled with an assortment of gypsies, beggars, vagrants, fortune tellers, quack doctors and those who practised charming and witchcraft — two arts that were slow to vanish in Cornwall. For the entertainment of the milling throng there were always plenty of side shows, amusements, wrestling matches, athletic events and strong beer on sale at numerous booths.

On 8 May there was the now famous Furry (meaning 'festival') day at Helston, when long processions of dancers made their way along the streets in and out of shops. At midsummer, 23 June, bonfires were lit all across Cornwall, and dancing, singing and drinking continued late into the warm summer night.

The Furry Dance is traditionally held in Helston, Cornwall, on 8 May. Here it is being re-enacted at a Cornish Festival (Kernewek Lowender) on Yorke Peninsula, South Australia.

Despite the Methodist adherence of so many of the people, they were also renowned as heavy drinkers. Public houses, or Kiddleywinks as they were sometimes called, dispensed cheap beer, in addition to brandy or gin frequently smuggled in from France. The publican also provided entertainment such as wrestling bouts or cock-fights, which attracted good crowds.

Because there were many things which made Cornishmen different from the English, it was not surprising that they were recognised as a distinctive human collectivity or, as we would now say, an ethnic group. (Max Weber in *Theories of Society* defines an ethnic group as 'a human collectivity based on an assumption of common origin, real or imaginary'.) One of their customs earned them a nickname that became internationally recognised: they were called Cousin Jacks, presumably because they addressed many of their kin as Cousin and also because one of their common Christian names was John (or Jack). The female counterparts were called Cousin Jennies.

The following chapters examine aspects of Cousin Jacks and Jennies who emigrated to Australia during the nineteenth century. There is one practical problem, however. Because they were nearly always labelled simply 'English' on shipping lists and in censuses (unlike the Irish, Scots or Welsh), it is not possible to say exactly how many of them went to Australia; but estimates would have to range in the tens of thousands. Philip Payton, in his doctoral thesis, The Cornish in South Australia, concluded that about 13 700 Cornish immigrants came to South Australia alone between 1836 and 1886, the last year of assisted immigration. Emigration from Cornwall still continues, but nowadays Cornish people who land in Australia are not as readily distinguished from other English-born as their nineteenth-century forebears. The years 1840 to 1880 were the period of greatest Cornish migration and it was then that the archetypal Cousin Jack was widely recognised as ethnic.

Although the precise numbers of Cornish emigrants are not known, two things are clear: most of them went to South Australia and most of them were miners. The latter statement is easily checked from those shipping lists which, contrary to the norm, did specify an emigrant's county of origin. Thus, for the period 1854 to 1858, the shipping lists for assisted immigrants to South Australia did specify Cornish people and, at the same time, gave their occupations. In this period, 1137 miners emigrated and the next largest occupational category was 117 agricultural labourers.

2 The Cornish Miner

Long before the Romans, Saxons or Normans conquered parts of England, Cornwall was both known and frequented for its mineral wealth. The earliest metal produced was tin, but subsequent mining operations proved that the country was rich in copper and lead.

Much of Cornwall is made up of massive granite and slate stones. Tin was found in the granite, the slate stone contained lead, and copper was often discovered at or near the junction of the two rock units. In all cases the ores were in veins, or lodes, and sophisticated mining methods were required to extract payable ore.

In the eighteenth century, a sizeable section of Cornwall's population worked in the mines. They were skilled at sinking shafts or driving levels. By 1841 miners were estimated to be 27 000 strong and, when their families were included, some 87 000 persons were directly dependent upon mining operations for their livelihood. (The total population was about 300 000.) By that time, copper miners outnumbered those who worked in all other mines.

Cornish miners had a rigid hierarchy of command in their workforce, with the lowest rank consisting of women and boys. The former were called bal-maidens, 'bal' being Cornish for a mine, and the latter were known as picky-boys. Both groups worked at the surface on the menial tasks of crushing the ore with hammers (usually done by the women) and picking the good ore from the useless country rock (usually done by the boys).

The next rank up the hierarchy were the tutmen, who worked on simple excavations. They sank shafts and put in levels, all measurements being done in running fathoms. Payment was for the total amount of material shifted and it made little difference to the tutmen whether they were shifting the lode or useless country rock.

Superior to the tutmen were the tributers, who operated as much as possible on the lode. They worked two-month periods, or 'takes', which began with 'setting day' when an arrangement was made with the mine management to work a 'pitch' at a price of so many shillings for each pound's worth of ore brought to the surface, treated and sold. Tributers were always bargainers and usually worked within the range of four shillings to thirteen shillings in the pound, depending upon the quality of ore in the lode.

This sketch first appeared in 1842, in Cyrus Redding's Illustrated Itinerary of Cornwall. *It shows typical features of a Cornish mine in the 1840s. There is an engine house, and a horse whim (left) and a rope whim for hauling ore to the surface. In the foreground are women ('bal maidens') breaking up the ore with hammers.*

Bargaining for a price was done with the next highest officer in the chain of command, namely a mine captain. Officers with this exalted title were usually miners who had worked their way up through the ranks and had a good working knowledge of the value of the ores in the mine. They established a price and haggled with tributers before a firm bargain was made. Captains were answerable to the mine management, usually one or a number of capitalists, who had purchased the rights to a mine from a landowner. They were known as adventurers.

The mining districts of Cornwall were located in three areas. The western included the parish of St Just and its near neighbourhood, which is the far south-western tip of England. The midlands fields covered a wide area from Hayle on the west coast to near Fowey on the east coast: its major mining towns were Camborne, Redruth, St Agnes and St Austell. Eastern mining activities centred around Liskeard and Callington, near the border with Devon.

Cornish miners in the early decades of the nineteenth century had diseases peculiar to their job and a life span that frequently did not exceed forty years. The two great causes of their ill-health were impure air and climbing ladders. The former was the result of poor ventilation in the mines. Sometimes as many as 600 men worked in one level deep below the surface. The lack of any forced replenishment of air meant that the atmosphere they breathed quickly became contaminated, so much so that the miners' candles would frequently be extinguished because of lack of oxygen. Furthermore, after blasting took place, the air was charged with minute dust particles which the workers inhaled in great volumes. The disease phthisis, contamination of the lungs, affected all able-bodied men who spent more than five years in the mines. If they worked for longer periods underground they grew noticeably paler and emaciated until eventually, racked with coughing and congestion in the chest, they died at early ages.

Apart from the daily doses of impure air, the miners had to contend with hours of ladder-climbing, going down to reach their pitch at the start of the day's work, or, more critically, going up to the surface when their work was completed. Frequently they climbed hundreds of metres at the end of a tiring day and passed from a hot, damp, impure atmosphere at the bottom to a cold, wet atmosphere at the surface. This brought daily strain on the heart and chest which progressively weakened their bodies and, along with the problems of the impure air, contributed further to their early deaths.

The daily meal of the miners while they were working did nothing to assist them in their health problems. It consisted of a coarse unleavened pasty containing perhaps a few pieces of turnip or an apple or two. Occasionally it was sweetened with a few raisins or currants, but often there was no filling at all and the miners digested nothing but heavy pastry. If they were working near the surface it was possible to ascend at about the dinner hour for their pasties to be heated at a forge, but if they worked well below the surface the meal was always eaten cold.

Connected with every mine there was a benefit society or a sick club. For a payment of sixpence a week to the club, a miner had the benefit of medical attention if he was ill or if he suffered from any accident. For a further ninepence a week, all the members of his family received the equivalent of modern medical insurance. Funeral expenses were defrayed out of the same fund, which also provided a lump sum to a woman and her family in the event of her husband's death while working in the mines.

Housing for the miners was often very inferior. Families tended to live in two-roomed stone cottages, sometimes enlarged to four rooms when the children grew up. Some cottages were very well built by young miners after they married, and it was frequently a matter of pride that miners were also good stonemasons. But many cottages were poorly maintained and, as they aged, they were little better than hovels, with damp, mouldy walls and thin, rotting thatched roofs. A writer in the *Morning Chronicle*, a newspaper read in Cornwall in the 1850s, cited the case of one such cottage in which fourteen people slept in one room. When asked how many beds they had to sleep on the writer was told that the room 'was all bed'.

The same writer expressed the opinion that miners, as a class, sacrificed to a great extent their domestic comforts to their inordinate love of clothes. To build a good cottage required an expenditure of £40 to £50, a large sum of money which was only obtained after many years of hard saving from wages that averaged little better than 15 shillings

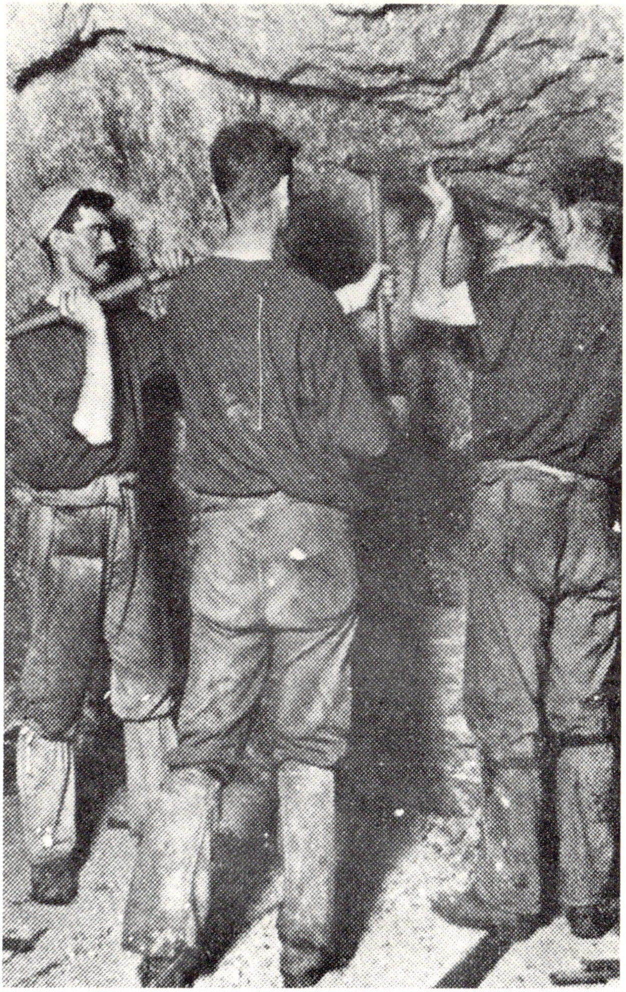

This 'staged' scene was photographed to illustrate the mining method common in Cornwall. One man (at the right here) held a drill steel; his two companions drove it into the rock face with alternate blows of their mallets. Later the drill hole was plugged with explosives and fuses were lit. In this way the ore was broken so that it could be hauled to the surface.

per week. Instead of doing this, many families spent their wages on material for clothes. This was made easy for them by 'tally men' or itinerant dealers who moved about the mining districts selling goods at high prices but taking payments by weekly or monthly instalments. The miners at church on a Sunday were usually attired in fine broadcloth and their wives paraded in great finery. The appearance belied the fact that their homes were often dens more resembling pigsties than human abodes.

Many married miners had small plots of land adjacent to their cottages. The plots, which were seldom bigger than the average suburban house lot in Australia today, were used to grow food to supplement a family's diet. Potatoes formed the main crop, as these gave the heaviest yield and also could be stored to last through winter. The humble potato was very important to the Cornish miner, and even the rotten ones were kept and fed to pigs which many families kept.

The mining population tended to be badly educated but deeply religious. Before the 1840s very few mine children received any formal education, and what schooling some did receive was generally a little of the three Rs and generous doses of religion at Sunday schools. Such schools were conducted in chapels of the Methodists, by far the most popular religious grouping amongst the mining fraternity.

The Methodist movement was started by John and Charles Wesley who advocated a religious life that was 'lived by rule and method', a saying that led to the title of Methodists. Beginning in 1743, the Wesleys visited Cornwall almost every summer until 1789. They spent most of their time in the mining districts and toiled extremely hard to win over the simple Cornish people, who had long been disenchanted with the Church of England because it was dominated by the wealthy landowners and shopkeepers of the county.

John Wesley's fame as a preacher grew and miners gathered year by year in ever-increasing numbers to listen to him. The parish of Gwennap was one of his favoured areas to visit and, in a deep tiered amphitheatre which had once been excavated by miners, Wesley spoke to thousands. The Gwennap Pit, as it was called, is still a renowned Methodist preaching place and an annual service has been held there every Whitsunday since Wesley's death.

Strong, emotional preaching was a basic characteristic of Methodism and, when its influence spread throughout Cornwall, dozens of earnest mining men strove to emulate the style and the impact of John Wesley. None was more effective than the legendary Billy Bray, the self-styled 'King's son'. Billy's grandfather was one of the earliest followers of Wesley and Billy grew up in a deeply religious household. For most of his life he was semi-illiterate but his parents and grandparents gave him a sound knowledge of the Bible. He decided when he was twenty-nine that he wanted to spread God's word amongst his fellow-miners and thereafter he used his strong lungs and spellbinding rhetorical powers at religious services all over Cornwall. His pulpit performances were a mixture of shouting, singing, dancing and fiery exhortations, interspersed with sermons that were liberally sprinkled with mining metaphors. He had enormous energy: he worked normal eight-hour mining shifts and then, on Sundays, for forty years, he walked all over the county preaching, building chapels and saving souls.

To thousands of Cornish miners, Billy Bray was God's agent on earth. They packed his meetings, sang lustily during his hymns and punctuated his prayers and sermons with frequent emotional outbursts of their faith, 'Glory, Glory', 'God be praised' and 'God bless 'ee Billy'.

Because the Methodist movement had very little financial support, it was not able to employ many preachers, nor was it able to build elaborate churches. Instead 'local preachers' of the Billy Bray type came forward and voluntary labour built small 'preaching houses' or chapels out of cob (clay and straw) or local stone. Leaders in the mining community, notably the captains, frequently became the preachers and also the building supervisors for the simple chapels, many of which still stand in the landscape of Cornwall today.

The Methodist movement began as a group or a 'society' within the Church of England but, in 1795, four years after the death of John Wesley, it formed a separate church. In the next twenty years there were a series of schisms that divided the movement into splinter groups, three of which were Wesleyan Methodists, Primitive Methodists and Bible Christians. (These groups eventually reunited under the single name Methodist in the early years of the twentieth century. In 1977 the Methodist church became part of the Uniting Church, a union of Presbyterians, Congregationalists and Methodists.)

Methodist chapels were a common building of the mining landscapes of Cornwall but they were overshadowed and outnumbered in the nineteenth century by the buildings which housed the engines for the mines. Cornish engineers developed mine engines over a long period and eventually developed a steam-operated pump engine which became internationally accepted as the best available for raising water from great depths at low cost. It consisted of a steam cylinder coupled to the end of a long rocking beam overhead. From the beam a long line of plunger pumps descended into the shaft of the mine. The beam projected from a stone engine house at a point high above the shaft and worked slowly but powerfully at about eight strokes per minute. Dozens of stone engine houses with their adjacent chimneys dotted the mining areas and many of them worked non-stop for decades, keeping shafts and levels clear of water. The foundries that made the engines, notably Harveys at Hayle, became famous for their products and, during the second half of the nineteenth century, supplied mining companies throughout the world.

In the early years of the nineteenth century there was plenty of work for copper miners in Cornwall, but by about 1840 there were signs that the copper lodes were being worked out. The year 1856 was the highest point of copper production in the county, and thereafter output declined dramatically; with it came increasing unemployment and crippling poverty.

For the destitute poor there were usually two alternatives. Firstly they could apply for positions in 'workhouses' which were a form of unemployment relief. However, the avowed policy of these places was to make work so unpleasant, and so poorly paid, that anybody who submitted to it was constantly looking to escape from it to any other available work. The second alternative was emigration and here the most attractive possibilities were the mines opening up in the New World, including Australia.

In the second half of the nineteenth century, the hard-rock miners of Cornwall spread all over the world, leading to another popular saying

One of the many stone buildings in Cornwall that once housed a beam engine. This one is two kilometres south of the old mining town, Camborne.

of the time — 'at the bottom of every hole in the ground you will find a Cornishman'. Copper mines, tin mines, lead mines and gold mines, in places as remote as Newfoundland, Cuba, Peru, New Caledonia, New Zealand and India, all employed Cousin Jack miners.

This bronze plaque (in Queen's Square, Moonta, South Australia) commemorates the part played by Cornish miners in settling the area. The candle in the helmet was kept in place by moist clay.

Australia received thousands of Cousin Jack miners who established themselves in the country and made an enormous contribution to our mineral development. They were an ethnic minority recognised for traits which may be summarised as follows:

They were skilled miners. They knew how to sink shafts, to timber shafts, to handle explosives, to operate — and build, if necessary — mine machinery, to assess the value of ores and to prospect for new deposits.

They were devout Methodists. Most of them were Wesleyan Methodists, but many also were Bible Christians or Primitive Methodists. Their religion was evident very often in their Biblical names, as for example in Malachi Deeble, Joshua Skinner, Methusalah Tregonning, Absalom Tonkin, Joseph Jolly, Israel Bennett, Jacob Burrows, Isaac Killicoat, Gabriel Faull and Solomon Jewell.

They spoke a Cornish dialect and used words common to their kind alone. Thus mines were 'bals', abandoned mines were 'knacked bals', mine officers were 'captains', a working in a mining area was a 'wheal', a work shift in a mine was a 'coor', courtship amongst young people was 'sparkin''.

They had distinctive interests, such as a love of festivals, an interest in wrestling and athletic contests and a love of singing. Other features of their lifestyle included eating pasties (and other Cornish foods such as saffron buns), cultivating food crops (which could extend to farming if the opportunity ever arose for them to make enough money to buy some land), a willingness to build their own houses, and a readiness to move on if and when a mine closed down or a new, richer deposit was opened up.

3 The Emigration Process

Cornish people began to emigrate to Australia in ones and twos as soon as immigrant ships were available. But what is popularly referred to as the Great Migration in Cornwall occurred between the years 1840 and 1880 and coincided with the decline in copper mining. Most of the emigrants were copper miners — often young, single men — but at the same time people with other occupations such as agricultural labourers, quarrymen, engine drivers and engineers also left Cornwall. A few of the wealthy upper classes went abroad and some settled in Australia; but frequently these people were either land speculators, or people who had been advised to live in the warm dry parts of Australia for the benefit of their health. Consumption and general diseases of the chest were common in Cornwall and it was a popular notion that life in Australia could alleviate such illnesses.

A good example of the life many of them wished to leave behind is provided by an autobiographical sketch given by Richard Best in the *Australian Christian Commonwealth* newspaper in 1911:

> I was born at St Dennis on October 8, 1847. My parents were poor. Father's wage was one shilling per day and out of this we paid house rent and fuel. Readers will therefore judge how our family of seven fared. I have tramped thousands of miles on errands, for each of which I would receive at most a penny, possibly a halfpenny and at times a crust.
>
> The conditions of our home necessitated my going to work at the early age of seven. I was engaged as a cowboy and my employer's responsibility to me was the payment of twopence per day and my dinner.

Australia had assisted immigration schemes which were attractive to impoverished miners and agricultural labourers. After 1831 some of the revenue which was obtained from land sales was used to bring out migrants, and the colonies of New South Wales and South Australia (after 1836) devised schemes to attract people to their shores. Victoria, after it separated from New South Wales in 1851, also had assisted immigration schemes. Each colony nominated the class of immigrant it needed and employed agents in Britain to recruit people.

Although the Cornish were attracted to all the colonies, the greatest overall migration was to South Australia where copper mines were opening up at the same time as they were closing down in Cornwall. Victoria attracted many people direct from Cornwall during the gold rush period and there are isolated examples of direct immigration to mining areas in Queensland, New South Wales and Tasmania. However, the most sustained migration was to places like Kapunda, Burra, Wallaroo and Moonta, the copper towns of South Australia.

There was a variety of reasons why the Cornish came and two, job-seeking and health problems, have already been suggested. There was also the spirit of adventure that drove young men in particular to visit other parts of the world, and this was an important factor when gold discoveries were being made in New South Wales and Victoria during the 1850s. But the most effective single factor that 'pushed' many people into migration was a letter from the colonies describing, in glowing terms, the economic richness of the new land.

Immigration agents knew the value of a good letter home: they actively solicited them and inserted them in English papers. A special publication of the late 1840s, *South Australian News*, was printed in London and widely distributed in Cornwall. It contained many glowing comments, such as the following, extracted from a letter written in 1848 by a Peter Medler who lived in Adelaide:

> Brother and sister, and neighbours, we wish to let you know what a rich and splendid province this is. There are mines in the province that are worth all Cornwall.

A letter from John Oats to his brother in Cornwall in 1847 made the following comments:

> Here is the place to live. The dogs have got more beef and mutton than ever we could get in England; if you could see how we are living you would not stop home a day.

Samuel Robins from Penryn emigrated in 1838. In 1847 he wrote to his sister at home thus:

> You remind me of my promise to return in ten years. I was young and foolish when I uttered that speech and I hope you will not expect me to leave a country like this.

The organisation of assisted immigration to Australia was done by emigration commissioners. They made public statements which pointed out that the funds for carrying emigrants to the colonies came from colonial revenues and that in the administration of the scheme they were bound to look exclusively to colonial interests. It was their duty to consider only how the largest number of emigrants most suited to the wants of the colonies were to be sent out, and they could not accept candidates merely because they were in distress or unable to procure employment.

The commissioners stated that they engaged first-class vessels which were dispatched from Southampton, Plymouth and Birkenhead. At these ports the commissioners had depots fitted expressly for the reception of emigrants, who were lodged and fed, free of charge, from the date of their embarkation order until they embarked. Notice was given that the ships were fitted out with a proper regard for the health and comfort of the emigrants as well as for the preservation of good order. The single men occupied the fore-part of the ship, next to them were the married couples and children in the middle of the vessel, and the single women had a distinct compartment in the after-part of the ship. A surgeon-superintendent was appointed for the medical care of the emigrants. The single women were placed in the care of a matron and, when practicable, a schoolmaster was appointed for the benefit of adults as well as children.

On reaching the colony none of the emigrants was bound in any way to the government, or required to make any payment in return for their passages. All emigrants were at liberty to choose their own employers and to make their own bargains for wages.

Emigration agents in the employ of the commissioners travelled throughout Cornwall and some sub-agents were permanently based in the large towns. With the aid of posters, advertisements in newspapers, and public meetings they endeavoured to tell all those who were interested the facts about emigrating to Australia.

A standard emigration form made it clear that not everybody would automatically gain an assisted passage to the antipodes. Eligible candidates had to be in the habit of working for wages and were to be sober, industrious, of good moral character, in good health, free from all mental and bodily defects and must have been vaccinated or had the smallpox.

There were categories of ineligible candidates: persons who had not arranged with their creditors; persons in business or intending to set up business in the colony for themselves, to buy land or to resort to the goldfields; persons in the habitual receipt of parish relief; families with more than two children under seven or more than three children under ten; widowers and widows with young children; parents without all their children under eighteen; children under eighteen without their parents; husbands without their wives; wives without their husbands; single women over thirty-five; single women who had given birth to illegitimate children and single men over forty.

Clearly the emigration commissioners had no thought for modern concepts such as 'equal opportunity' and 'non-discrimination' on the grounds of age, sex, race, etc.

Many of the regulations were circumvented by false statements. Thus many children's ages were 'altered' to fit the regulations and there were cases when families with more than the permitted number of children transferred some of their children to small families travelling on the same ship.

If a prospective emigrant was able to declare himself and his family as eligible candidates, his application form needed four signatures in addition to his own. Two were required from 'respectable householders', one from a physician or surgeon as an indication of good health, and one from a clergyman. The application form could then be submitted to an emigration agent.

If the emigration commissioners approved the application, the eligible candidates received an approval circular and then some months later their embarkation orders which indicated the name of the ship they would sail in and its port of departure.

The voyages to Australia in nineteenth-century sailing ships were experiences that all emigrants remembered with mixed feelings for the rest of their lives. In the 1840s the emigrant ships were frequently small, cramped and dirty, but later they improved and emigration commissioners seemed genuinely to have tried to engage the best ships available. Sea-sickness and storms provided the most vivid memories for most emigrants, but many voyages were also plagued by sickness on board, by shortages of food and by overbearing, unsympathetic ship's officers.

There are many diaries, and some books, available in Australian libraries that tell the stories of emigrants' voyages to the colonies. From these sources one typical account has been selected. It tells of two brothers, Christopher and Joseph, and their journey from Cornwall to South Australia in 1864 in the *Adamant.*

The brothers received their embarkation orders in June of 1864: their ship was due to sail from Plymouth on or about July 14.

At Plymouth their two-day stay in the depot was punctuated by new arrivals with every train. Other Cornishmen came from the south-west but they were far outnumbered by English, Irish and Scots who arrived from the north. In the meantime the *Adamant* had been loading cargo in London before making her way down the Channel to Plymouth. Beneath the steerage cabins the crew stowed a variety of goods needed in the colony: 45 tonnes of smithy coals, 50 casks of cement, 200 casks of bottled beer, 150 casks of stout, 7 cases of hams and bacons, 49 307 firebricks for the Wallaroo smelters, bars, hoop iron, 150 kegs of nails, 450 bundles of wire, 50 iron tanks, 88 cases of galvanised iron.

The *Adamant* was a barque of 740 tonnes, a common cargo carrier that had been converted to an emigrant ship. The master, B. Lodwick, had recently been appointed a Lieutenant in the Royal Naval Reserve. He had a reputation as a kindly commander who usually took his wife on voyages with him, a practice that raised no objections from the emigration commissioners. The other first-class cabins on the *Adamant* in July 1864 were filled by Miss Charlotte Hooper, the matron in charge of the single women emigrants, and by Dr William G. Gunn, the Surgeon-Superintendent. Dr Gunn was a veteran of more than ten emigration voyages and was highly respected by the commissioners, particularly as five of his voyages had been completed without a death on board.

The *Adamant* berthed at Plymouth on 11 July, and in the next four days 368 emigrants were checked by the government health inspectors and then given permission to go on board. The ship was permitted to carry 331 'statute adults' and the final head count showed 302 adults and 66 children under the age of 14 including several babes in arms. The total was computed to be the equivalent of 329½ 'statute adults'.

Christopher and Joseph found, as they expected, that they were accommodated in the fore-part of the ship. They had not expected that they would be sharing their quarters with 119 other single men and that their living area would be a regulation fifteen square feet (about one and a half square metres) which included a bed. The brothers shared a two-tier berth made up of bunks knocked together with coarse planks. There was just over half a metre on all sides between their bunks and those of the neighbours. Most of the single men found the crowded quarters claustrophobic but the brothers, and the twenty-one other single Cornish miners on the ship, accepted the conditions as no worse than working in narrow drives hundreds of feet beneath the grass.

At the rear of the ship were 101 single women, most of whom were destined to become domestic servants in the colony. The remaining group, married couples and children, were accommodated with a little more free space in the centre of the ship. Two hundred and twenty of the emigrants came from English counties, forty-eight came from Scotland and one hundred came from Ireland.

On 16 July the *Adamant* was taken about five kilometres outside the Plymouth harbour by a towing-tug and, when the connecting lines were dropped and the tug moved away, the two brothers severed their connection with England forever.

The run down the English Channel began with a fair wind, but after the first day it freshened to a stiff breeze and the ship began to roll and pitch in a manner that the passengers found alarming. Amongst the single men the first few hours of sailing had been spent in high spirits with much jocularity, but as the day ended everybody became more subdued, and although few would admit it, most of them were struggling with the first signs of seasickness. Soon after the evening meal the spewing began. It spread rapidly from berth to berth until no one was left untouched by the retching, the mess and, above all, the stench. To go on deck with the pitching and rolling was unthinkable and there was nowhere to be sick except the privies or their berths. The privies were quickly clotted with vomit, buckets and baskets were filled to overflowing and bedding was frequently fouled not only with the occupant's own vomit but with the spray and spittle of a neighbour's upheavals. And through all this, the passengers who had chosen the low berths were constantly at the mercy of their ailing companions above.

This horrendous first night of sickness was common to most emigrant voyages. It left the steerage areas with a persistently foul odour for the rest of the voyage and it took many days of fine weather thereafter, which the *Adamant* fortunately had, to restore the passengers to good spirits and normal eating habits.

For the first month of the voyage, light weather conditions restricted the ship to 50–75 kilometres per day and although the commander found this speed frustrating, communication with passing ships indicated that no others were faring better. Thus, when on the *Adamant's* fortieth day of sailing, the *Margaret Pugh*, en route to Calcutta, was spoken to, it was forty-seven days from Plymouth. The equator was crossed on 14 August and soon after, the ship was becalmed for three days. The passengers spent their time fishing and reading, and on a few occasions the commander permitted a boat to be lowered over the side and parties indulged in some strenuous rowing across the calm seas, which was an invigorating exercise and a refreshing break from a monotonous daily routine. On Christopher's twentieth birthday, 29 August, the ship crossed the Tropic of Capricorn and was making good time towards rounding the Cape of Good Hope. Soon afterwards the

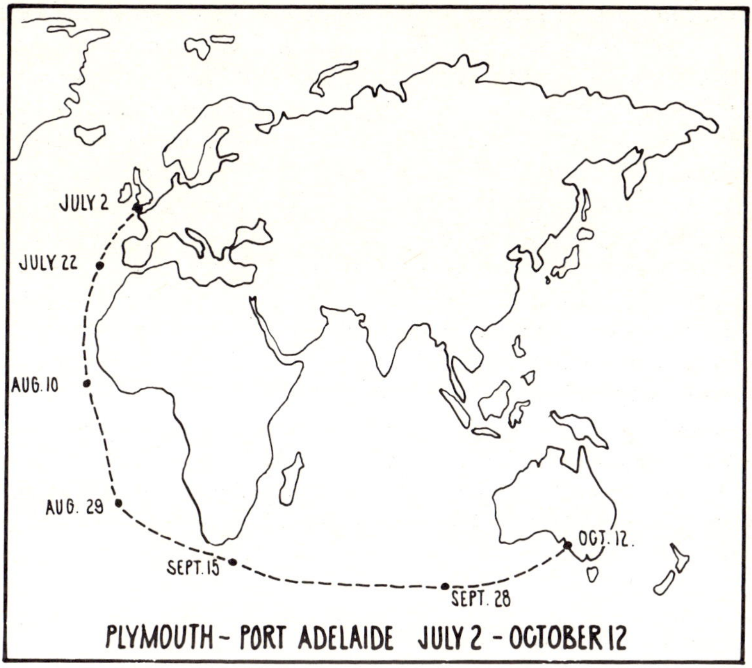

The route taken by the Adamant *in 1864.*

winds shifted westerly, the weather became cold and table-top icebergs were sighted frequently on the southern horizon.

The crew of the *Adamant* were expert fishermen, so the ship's provisions were constantly supplemented by fresh fish. The boatswain was skilful with a harpoon and it was a favourite form of ship's entertainment to watch him bring on board porpoises and small sharks. South of the Cape, albatrosses frequently kept the ship company and one of the first that was sighted was shot by the commander. It flopped into the sea where it was devoured by several other albatrosses that immediately appeared on the scene. A day later one was shot that collapsed on the deck, where it was measured and found to be 8 feet 10 inches (2.7 metres) in its wing span. As the ship moved along under a stiff breeze and got further into southern waters, the birds became more numerous, frequently landing on the deck; they were comically clumsy in their attempts to get themselves launched again. Amongst the single men it was considered great sport to catch the clumsy birds, the record for the voyage being seven in one day with the largest bird having a twelve-foot (3.7-metre) wing span.

Late in September, in latitude 47°S, the ship experienced its only severe gale for the voyage. The weather was bitterly cold, snow squalls constantly beat upon the ship for three days, the sea came over the side in great quantities and, in the fore-part of the ship where the pitching and rolling seemed likely to break up the ship at any moment, the floor was awash with icy water. Christopher and Joseph, along with dozens of others, tied themselves into their bunks and prayed for the Lord's speedy deliverance from the storm.

Late on the third day of the bad weather, the ship shuddered under a particularly strong windburst and then abruptly ran into a calm. The full press of sail collapsed momentarily and then the wind swept in again with a force that split the fore-topsail. The mizzentopmast came down with a crash, the mainyard was sprung and some of the headstays were parted. In this battered state the ship rode out the rest of the storm, which fortunately abated the next day.

Lieutenant Lodwick inspected the damage and consulted the ship's carpenter about the need for repairs. The carpenter had many friends amongst the emigrants and a team of skilled workers was quickly organised. They set to with a will, pleased to be doing something constructive after two months of inactivity, and the damage was repaired in less than two days, during which time the weather fortunately remained fine and the sea was relatively calm.

In the early days of October, when the ship was sailing south of the Great Australian Bight, the course was altered from due east to more north-east; soon afterwards, first the crew and then the passengers began to smell land, a smell not unlike freshly tilled soil. Then patches of seaweed began to appear and soon dozens of patches were passing the ship each hour. Every person on board was alert for the first sight of the Australian continent and Christopher and Joseph spent hour after hour near the bow of the ship peering towards the northern horizon.

Then, early on 8 October, several crew members began pointing to a brown smudge on the horizon and by mid-morning it was clearly visible to everybody on board. The ship's officers calculated that this was the western end of Kangaroo Island, that large island that guards the entrance to the Gulf St Vincent on the shores of which is Adelaide, the capital of South Australia.

In the next few days the *Adamant* rounded the western end of Kangaroo Island, sailed through Investigator Strait and, with land usually visible on both sides, proceeded northwards up the Gulf to the lightship near the mouth of the river that leads into Port Adelaide. At the lightship the *Adamant* was met by a small tug and preparations were made to tow the ship into the river. At the same time a shipping inspector and a colonial health inspector boarded the *Adamant* and proceeded to examine the state of the vessel and the health of its occupants. Summaries of their reports were subsequently published in the South Australian *Register*, along with a list of the ship's passengers. The report of the shipping inspector complimented the commander on the 'ship's superior trim on arrival' and the health inspector's report noted that the voyage had been completed without a death on board.

The *Adamant* was towed into the Port Adelaide river on 13 October and there it anchored in the stream about fifty metres offshore. The passengers were disembarked in small groups in rowing boats and Joseph and Christopher spent several hours of frustrating delay waiting for their turn to climb into a boat. Eventually, just as the sun was setting, the two brothers were taken ashore and they placed their feet on land for the first time in more than twelve weeks.

The *Adamant* was one of eight emigrant ships to South Australia in 1864. Its eighty-six-day voyage was the fastest for the year, the average time being ninety-seven days, and it was the only ship in that year which completed its voyage without a death on board. The preceding ship, the *Art Union*, had twelve deaths from measles and whooping cough. The *Adamant* landed 370 emigrants, including two babies born on the voyage, and these people were part of a total of 2647 emigrants for the year. From the total, 463 came from Cornwall and 142 gave their occupations as miners.

4 The Advance Scouts

The site that was chosen in 1836 for the first permanent settlement in South Australia was on a small stream which flows across plains about twenty kilometres wide descending from the foothills of the Mount Lofty Ranges. The site became the town of Adelaide, ultimately the capital city of the colony.

The ranges became an early source of timber for the town and even the most casual observers visiting the stringybark forests in the gullies and ridges near Adelaide noted that the trees grew in thin soils that covered old and resistant rocks. In August of 1838 a bullock dray which was being driven up a hillside disturbed some loose rock and, in the fresh broken surfaces underneath, the tell-tale green and blue stains of copper ore were noted. The land had recently been surveyed as section 295 and was owned by the Colonial Treasurer, Osmond Gillies, whose name had been given to the neighbouring deep valley known as Glen Osmond.

For unknown reasons Gillies did not establish a mine on the site, but news of the discovery attracted the attention of two new arrivals in the colony, Messrs Thomas and Hutchins who had been miners in Cornwall. They obtained work as labourers in the city but found time to prospect in the ranges near the original copper discovery. In February 1841 they found a rich silver-lead lode and a company was formed to mine it. It was named Wheal Gawler after the Governor of the colony, George Gawler.

Work was commenced immediately, and in April 1841 forty boxes of ore from the mine were sent to England. From 1845 the ore was smelted before being exported and a small smelting furnace was operating in Rundle Street, which is now one of the principal streets in

This Cornish-built chimney, which dates from the 1840s, is on the slopes above Glen Osmond in South Australia. It is part of the first metalliferous mining area in Australia where there was a recognisable concentration of Cornish immigrants.

Adelaide's central business district. The smelter was the first of its kind in Australia and the Wheal Gawler was the first metalliferous mine worked in Australia.

The Wheal Gawler was worked spasmodically by a South Australian company until 1846, when it was sold and worked by a German company until 1851.

In 1843 a second mine in the Glen Osmond area, the Wheal Watkins, was opened on a section of land to the south of Wheal Gawler and, in 1846, Osmond Gillies opened a mine he called Glen Osmond Union. To work this he engaged J.B. Pascoe to be the mine captain and brought his family plus ten other mining families out from Cornwall.

Several other small mines were opened in the vicinity of Glen Osmond, the Enterprise in 1847, Finke's Mine in 1844, McFarlane's Mine in 1844, Wheal Hardy in 1848 and the Wheal Grainger in 1848.

None of the Glen Osmond mines was a lasting success but the area was one of the first in Australia where there was a recognisable concentration of Cornish people, all of whom depended upon the mines for their livelihood. A 'miners' village' existed as early as 1841 when there were at least three cottages occupying 11 hectares of land.

History has recorded only a few of the names of the Glen Osmond Cornishmen, but it is known that Captain Stephen Lean worked at Wheal Watkins and the Glen Osmond Union as a young man. George Prout, who came from Camborne, began a long career in the mining industry as a picky-boy at Glen Osmond and so did Stephen Carthew from Redruth. Other known Cornishmen were miners called Trewartha, Knucky, Ede, Veal, Mitchell, Odgers and Trethowan.

A second concentration of Cornishmen grew up at the Willunga slate quarries, thirty kilometres south of Adelaide, in the early 1840s. The slate was discovered in the hills above the town of Willunga in 1840 and by 1841 the commodity was being exported. Slate was quarried for the rest of the century and during peak periods there were more than 100 workmen operating in four quarries, Martin's, Bastian's, Bangor and Delabole.

The Cornish influence at Willunga was very strong. Delabole quarry was named after the famous quarry in North Cornwall. Martin's Quarry was owned by Thomas Martin, a Cornishman, and was originally opened up by two Cornish prospectors, Thomas Williams and Thomas Polkinghorne. Bastian's and Delabole quarries were owned by Sampson Bastian and Sampson Dawe respectively, both of Cornish descent. And the Bangor quarry which was named after the slate-producing district of North Wales had as one of its owners James Kernick from Trevena, Cornwall.

In the late 1840s Delabole had a village comprised almost entirely of Cornishmen who worshipped at their own Wesleyan chapel. However, the nearest 'kiddleywinks', one of which was appropriately named Cornwall Inn, were in nearby Willunga.

It was at Kapunda, eighty kilometres north of Adelaide, that copper was first discovered in large quantities in Australia. In 1843 Frances Dutton discovered rich green stains of copper carbonates while rounding up sheep. He reported that his first thoughts were that the deposit was 'beautiful green moss'. With a neighbour, Charles Bagot, Dutton quietly bought thirty-two hectares of land around the deposit. They then commenced mining and Bagot reported in his memoirs that he engaged Robert Nicholls, a Cornish miner, to work for a year on tribute. The mine was a success and it immediately attracted many Cornishmen in the colony who were experienced in mining. Many of them abandoned their jobs as agricultural labourers and moved to live and work at Kapunda.

Fifteen tonnes of Kapunda ore was shipped to Swansea in Wales early in 1844. When smelted it gave 26 per cent copper and created a favourable impression amongst mining men not only in Wales but also in Cornwall. A South Australian copper boom had begun and many miners in Cornwall started to take an interest in the development of the colony.

The Kapunda mine operated until 1878. In the early years the miners lived in wattle and daub cottages near the mine site. Although the majority of the workers underground were Cornish, there were also German miners, and a large force of Irish immigrants operated as teamsters carting the ore from the mine to Port Adelaide. In the 1850s a smelting plant was erected and this attracted a further ethnic group of workers, namely the Welsh, who in so many parts of Australia were to work in mining fields smelting the ore that the Cornish brought to the surface.

In 1848 a second-hand beam engine was brought to Kapunda from Cornwall, the first engine of its type to be erected in Australia. It was the forerunner of dozens of other engines that were to be installed in stone engine houses all over the continent.

The first two managers of the Kapunda mine were Irishmen, Captain Bagot, one of the original discoverers, and William Oldham. Thereafter the managers were Cornishmen, and this extended to not only the top captain's position but to lesser managerial positions which also carried the title of captain. Thus Captain Thomas Nicholls, a man with con-

An 1840s illustration of the Kapunda mine. Notice the horse whim for hauling the ore to the surface, and the line of 'picky boys' sorting the ore.

siderable mining experience in Cornwall, was appointed to take charge of the precipitate works at the mine. Captain Osborne managed the mine for some years and so did Captain Israel Bennett.

Israel Bennett had a characteristic that was typical of many Cornish mining specialists, particularly those that came to Australia. This was mobility, the willingness to move about from place to place in search of work, new mines, or opportunities for advancement. Bennett was born at Chacewater, near Truro, in Cornwall in 1834 and he commenced work in the copper mines when he was eleven years old. At sixteen he transferred to a lead mine in north Cornwall and at twenty-four he took charge of pumping and general engineering work at a copper mine in Devonshire. In 1860 when he was twenty-six he was appointed a captain at mines in Spain and stayed there for two years. He next moved to South Australia and was appointed general surface manager at Kapunda.

Bennett stayed at Kapunda for ten years but then accepted a position as a manager at the Mount Perry copper mines in Queensland. Here he stayed for sixteen years until he received an appointment as Government Inspector of Mines for the Central District of Queensland.

Throughout their thirty-five years of operation the Kapunda mines were only barely profitable. There were also a few nearby prospects which had brief periods of activity. Thus there was South Kapunda (Captain Henry Francis), North Kapunda and Wheal Gundry (Captain Gundry) and Lacamore (Captain John Rowe).

All the mines were serviced by the town of Kapunda which was laid out in the late 1840s. The Cornish who helped build the mines and the town never established themselves as a dominating concentration in the town; many of them left the area for the goldfields in Victoria in the 1850s and for the more secure mines at Wallaroo and Moonta in the 1860s and 1870s. However, there are still features in Kapunda which point to the Cornish occupation during the nineteenth century. Thus an old mine chimney, the captain's house and the ruins of the mine offices still stand overlooking the old mining area. The Methodist (now Uniting) Church is a prominent building in the town. It was originally built as a Wesleyan Methodist Church and was opened in 1858. There is also, still standing, an old building which was a Primitive Methodist Church opened in 1864.

Part of the town of Kapunda was laid out as the village of Helston, a name with many Cornish connections. And there is further evidence in the town in the form of some old miners' cottages that have a Cornish flavour about them and headstones in the public cemetery which indicate that Trevillicks, Trelawnys and Treloars, obviously Cornish people, lived and died in Kapunda last century.

The discovery of copper at Kapunda set off a spate of prospecting in other parts of the colony. In the remaining years of the 1840s several small mines were opened, and operations were begun at the major deposit at Burra (see Chapter 5).

Montacute mine, about twenty kilometres north of the Glen Osmond Mines, was in operation in 1844. The local Adelaide newspaper, the *Register,* reported that 'Arrangements made with Cornish miners for working it are . . . very liberal'. Captain Samuel Terrell was engaged to manage the mine.

To the east of Mount Barker, a prominent peak in the Mount Lofty Ranges, two groups applied for a special mineral survey of 20 000 acres (8100 hectares) of land in 1845. One group, called the Joint Applicants, consisted of a group of wealthy speculators living in South Australia. They eventually gained ownership of 3200 hectares. The other group was the South Australian Company, a pioneer land-purchasing company led by its manager, William Giles. The Company bought 4900 hectares. The area became known as the Mount Barker Mineral Survey and was to see the development of several small copper mines at Kanmantoo, Paringa and Callington (or Bremer). Cornishmen were brought to the area by both groups and they set about establishing small villages with Cornish names such as Callington and St Ives.

The chimney and powder magazine of the old Bremer mine, Callington, South Australia. The interesting circular magazine, built by Cornish craftsmen, has a National Trust plaque at the entrance.

Amongst the many Cornish people who settled on the survey, Captain Joseph Lean was one of the best known. He came to the colony in 1840 and worked as a captain for several years at the Glen Osmond mines. He was then engaged to prospect for the South Australian Company and he discovered the ore at the Kanmantoo mine in 1845.

When the South Australian Company acquired its portion of the mineral survey, Lean and his large family of seven sons and one daughter, plus other mining families, moved into the area and established a small village that was called Staughton. This grew into a typical Cornish miners' village and there was a well-beaten path from it to the Kanmantoo mine. Joseph Lean's family occupied several of the stone cottages which were built. James Lean was one occupant after he married the daughter of Captain Cornelius from the Paringa Mine. Sarah Lean also occupied a cottage when she married Henry Jackson, a miner and subsequently Staughton's storekeeper.

Almost as soon as the first cottages were built at Staughton, a Primitive Methodist Chapel was erected. William Snell, miner, Nicholas Brokenshire, miner and Abraham George, miner, were some of the early members of the chapel trust.

The mines in the Mount Barker Mineral Survey were active for about a decade but were never greatly prosperous. Many of the miners moved away to the Victorian goldfields, to the Burra mine and the Wallaroo and Moonta mines. Some hints of their occupation are easily seen at Callington and Kanmantoo today, but the little village of Staughton is no longer inhabited. There are a few stone ruins where it used to be. Thus it is an example of something that is repeated all over Australia, the death of a small village established by Cornishmen to service a promising mining area. When the mines were worked out, the village died and only small traces of its ruins can be found today.

Captain Richard Rodda was a prominent Cornish captain from the time he arrived in the colony in 1846. He was sent out by George Fife Angas, one of the founding fathers of the colony and one of its earliest large landowners. Rodda, who came from Penrice, near St Austell in Cornwall, brought a party of miners with him and was engaged to prospect and mine on the land owned by Angas in the Barossa Valley area. The group worked small shows at Greenock Creek and Lyndoch

Valley and in 1850 opened up Wheal Friendship near Williamstown and the North Rhine claim east of Angaston.

Richard Rodda laid out a small miner's village called Penrice after his birthplace. Unlike Staughton, Penrice has survived to this day and has become part of one of the well-known Barossa Valley towns, Angaston.

By 1850 the strength of the Cornish community in South Australia was such that a short-lived but influential 'Cornwall and Devon Society' was formed. The secretary was John Bentham Neales, an entrepreneur who made a fortune in the Burra mine, and its committee was dominated by mining captains, namely Captain Boundy, Burra Mine; Captain Cornelius, Paringa Mine; Captain Henry Francis, South Kapunda; Captain Gundry, North Kapunda; Captain Hammatt, Enterprise Mine; Captain Lean, Wheal Prosper; Captain Long, Wheal Acraman; Captain Mullett, Wheal Friendship; Captain Samuel Osborne, Burra; Captain J.B. Pascoe, Glen Osmond; Captain John Phillips, Worthing Mine; Captain Alfred Phillips, Reedy Creek; Captain Paull, Wheal Margaret; Captain Roach, Burra; Captain John Rowe, Wheal Barton; Captain Simmons, Wheal Maria; Captain Trewartha, Government Mineral Surveyor; Captain Trestrail, Phoenix Mine; Captain Terrell, Mary Consols; Captain Absolom Tonkin, Bremer Mine. Other committee members included a collection of Adelaide businessmen, three doctors and a solicitor.

The aims of the society were to encourage emigration from Cornwall and Devon, to watch over the interests of Devon and Cornish colonists, and to promote harmony and good feeling among them.

The Cornwall and Devon Society, like so many concerns in South Australia, languished and died during the big exodus of able-bodied men to the Victorian gold rushes in 1851.

While South Australia was establishing a strong Cornish community in the 1840s, there were also some Cornishmen being attracted to copper mines in New South Wales.

The earliest attempt to mine copper in New South Wales is thought to have been in 1844, and it is known that mines were being worked at

Copper Hill, near Molong in 1845. In 1847 copper was being extracted at Summerhill near Rockley and, in an official dispatch in 1849, Governor Fitzroy stated that copper mines were in operation near Yass and near Molong.

Mining operations at Summerhill continued successfully for many years and in 1853 one of the first examples of inter-colonial migration amongst copper miners occurred. There were to be many such migrations in the history of Australian mining and in most cases it was a movement of men from the established copper mines in South Australia to developing mines in other colonies.

Captain Hitchins, the manager of the Kapunda smelting works, was enticed to Summerhill in the 1850s with a very generous salary of £500 per year (at that time most miners were earning less than £100 per year). He was an experienced captain and mining engineer, having worked for nine years at copper mines in South America before coming to South Australia. At Summerhill he assessed the needs of the mine and immediately returned to South Australia, where he collected a party of miners. He also purchased a steam engine and machinery which was sent to Summerhill.

In 1850 one of the most successful of the early New South Wales copper mines was opened at what is today known as Byng, twenty kilometres east-south-east of Orange and forty-five kilometres from Bathurst. At the time of the discovery the area was known as Cornish Settlement because of the influence of one of New South Wales' best-remembered Cornishmen, William (Pastor) Tom.

Tom was born on a farm near Bodmin, Cornwall in 1791. In 1823, with his wife, three children, a nephew, a sister, her husband and their two children, he arrived in Sydney. The two families took up land eighteen kilometres from Orange in 1830 and Tom named his property 'Springfield'. Other Cornish settlers were attracted to the district and in 1842 a small stone church was built in the area by Cornish stonemasons. William Tom became the principal preacher in the church and earned the name 'Parson' Tom for his long and strenuous efforts at the pulpit.

When copper was discovered at Carangara a few kilometres away, Cornish Settlement was further enlarged by the arrival of groups of

Cornish miners brought direct from Cornwall to work the mine and later the reverberatory furnaces that were built to treat the ore.

In February 1851 the Bathurst correspondent to the *Sydney Morning Herald* reported that it was most gratifying to know that copper from Cornish Settlement had recently sold for £75/15/- per ton, 5/- per ton more than the price given for a parcel of South Australian copper which had been submitted at the same sale in Sydney. However, this richness did not last for many years and Cornish Settlement was not able to develop into a large copper mining district.

Many Cornish folk remained in the area and took up farming. George Hawke, for example, established a property he called 'Pendarves'. He died aged eighty in 1882 and Richard Grenfell, William Bishop and Nicholas Bray were other Cornishmen who lived beyond seventy years each and died at Cornish Settlement.

In 1851 E.H. Hargraves, the gold prospector, visited the Tom family at 'Springfield'. He showed William Tom how to build a cradle for washing gold and soon after William, with J.H.A. Lister, found nuggets in one of the nearby creeks. They wrote to Hargraves who hurried back and proclaimed the Ophir Goldfield, destined to become the site of the first Australian gold rush.

A few Cornish miners were also attracted to Western Australia, when some discoveries of copper and lead were made near Northampton in the late 1840s. There were two mining settlements, Wannerenooka and Gwalla, but the whole locality was known simply as 'The Mines' until the town of Northampton was surveyed in 1864. Captain Samuel Mitchell and a party of Cornish miners worked at 'The Mines' and Mitchell became a prominent citizen in the area. His old home, 'Chiverton House', is now a local museum that is the headquarters of the Northampton Historical Society.

5 The Burra Concentration

After the discovery of copper at Kapunda in South Australia, there were dozens of amateur prospectors working in the unopened lands of the colony, looking for telltale green and blue stains on rocks. Such stains usually indicated the presence of copper ore. In 1845, two shepherds working at different points along the Burra-Burra Creek, 150 kilometres north of Adelaide, made important discoveries. The existence of copper ore in the area was soon established and an interesting battle then took place to see who should own the land and thus mine the ore.

Because the land was outside the boundaries of prescribed settlement in South Australia, the only possible way it could be obtained was in the form of a special survey and purchase of 20 000 acres (8100 hectares) which would cost £20 000. Two rival groups managed jointly to raise the necessary money; they were nicknamed the 'Nobs' and the 'Snobs'. After the purchase was made, the land was divided in halves and each group drew lots. The Snobs, who had formed themselves into the South Australian Mining Association, obtained the northern half which was to become the Burra mine. The Nobs received the southern half, which proved to have very little copper and was eventually sold as the Princess Royal pastoral property.

The Snobs got a bonanza, a veritable 'Monster Mine', a name by which it was often known. Their first captain, Thomas Roberts, was transferred from the Montacute mine with nine other Cornish miners and by October 1845 they were raising 55 tonnes per week of copper ore that assayed more than 70 per cent copper.

As Ian Auhl has indicated in his *Burra Sketchbook*, the successful shareholders of the Monster Mines were not the Cornish miners but a collection of 'shopkeeping nobodies' from Adelaide who became copper kings with the bonanza profits of their mine. Their original £5 shares, of which there were 2464 in all, earned quarterly dividends of 200 per cent, and gave them financial security for life. Graham, an ironmonger, invested £2075 and secured an income of £16 000 a year; Paxton, a chemist, built a mansion on North Terrace, Adelaide and later sold it to the company secretary, Henry Ayers. The mansion still stands, a monument to Burra's profitability. Known as Ayers House, it is a restaurant and also the headquarters of the South Australian Branch of the National Trust. The enormous wealth from the mines contributed greatly to the economic stability of South Australia, which up until that time had been a struggling colony. The Cornish brought the wealth to the surface, but never shared handsomely in its distribution, for while the shopkeepers built mansions the miners built cottages and struggled along on wages of about 30 shillings a week.

Thomas Roberts was typical of many Cornish miners in that once he had made some money he gave up the hard work of mining and bought some land. Roberts bought an agricultural section sixteen kilometres north-east of Adelaide, called his farm Greenwith after his home locality in Cornwall, and helped build the Greenwith Primitive Methodist Chapel across the road from his farmhouse.

The enormous success of the Burra mine brought a heavy demand for large numbers of miners. Initially they came from mines already established. Many left Kapunda for Burra and the Montacute mines in the Adelaide Hills were almost deserted as miners and their families trekked north to the Monster Mine.

The South Australian Mining Association's secretary, Henry Ayers, became an active recruitment officer for the Burra mines. He also held shares in the mine and as a result became very wealthy. Later he was Premier of South Australia and Ayers Rock in the Northern Territory is named after him.

Ayers established a close relationship with J.B. Wilcocks, an emigration agent in Cornwall. Copies of many letters that Ayers sent to Wilcocks are still kept in the South Australian Archives and they show that Ayers persistently requested the recruitment of more and more miners. At one stage he was claiming to Wilcocks that he could employ

Many of the Cornishmen at the mines worked on the surface, as ore dressers, engine-men or labourers. This group at Burra in the 1860s was working as a road gang in the mining area. The man second from right is wearing a miner's helmet.

a thousand hands, consisting of miners, blacksmiths, engineers, carpenters and others employed at copper mines. Another time, he claimed that Burra was 'thirsting for labour' and in 1854 he offered Wilcocks a bounty of £2 per head for good Cornish miners.

Wilcocks was extremely successful, especially after Ayers made the £2 bounty offer. In the years 1854 and 1855 he sent 1600 Cornish migrants to the colony, mostly miners and their families.

Although the Burra mine also attracted Welsh smelters, German miners and Irish labourers and teamsters, it was the Cornish who were overwhelmingly the most numerous. Almost all the positions of responsibility went to Cornishmen. Thus the chief captain, or general superintendent as he was called, from 1847 until he retired in 1868 was Henry Roach who came from Redruth. In 1847 Captain Matthew Bryant was made second captain; Richard Goldsworthy from Bodmin became third captain and William Mitchell was fourth captain.

The engineers Peter Spargo and John Congdon were Cornishmen, and so was the chief clerk Mr Boswarna. Two Cornish masons, Ambrose Harris and Thomas Paynter, built most of the engine houses and chimney stacks for the mine.

As soon as the mine was proved and a large work force was assembled, operations were organised on typically Cornish lines. There were tribute and tutwork systems and survey days were set down as the first working day of each month. At the same time Ayers was writing long letters to Cornwall engaging agents to sell the copper (John Williams and Son of Truro), and mining authorities to supervise the purchase of machinery for the mine (Richard Hallett and Sons of London). He asked for tenders from Hayle and Perran foundries to supply engines, winding gear, chains, ore-crushing stamps and vast amounts of small equipment ranging from mining steels to iron nails.

The settlement at Burra was laid out along the Burra-Burra Creek, a watercourse that was usually dry for most of the year. Within four years of discovery there were more than 4000 people living near the mine. It was reported that because the laying out of townships and the building of cottages could not keep pace with the demand, some 2600 people were camped along the creek. Of these, many were miners who burrowed into the banks of the creek and constructed two or three rooms as a family home. A visitor to Burra in 1850 reported that some of the riverbank dwellings comprised four rooms joined by tunnels. Their chimneys protruded into the footpaths above and often proved a hazard to walkers. Some of the dwellings had substantial doors, glazed sashes and even shingle verandahs. A newspaper report of the time referred to them as 'grotto houses'.

When the creek flooded three times in 1851, many of the homes in the banks were washed away and numerous families lost all their possessions. A few grotto houses remained and, in recent years, these have been carefully preserved by the National Trust; they can be seen in Burra today.

A dugout or 'grotto house' excavated in the bank of the Burra Creek and preserved as a tourist attraction by the National Trust.

The South Australian Mining Association laid out its own town on its mining lease in 1846. Several hundred cottages were built for its miners and these were made available for renting. Many of the miners, particularly the Cornish, viewed the 'boss's town' with suspicion and preferred to have either a dugout along the creek or a stone cottage they could build themselves somewhere off the mining lease. The mine directors originally wanted to call their town Truro, an obvious reference to Cornwall, but finally settled for Kooringa, a corruption of Cooringa which was an Aboriginal name meaning she-oak and creek.

Because the South Australian Mining Association would not permit individual ownership of land and dwellings in its company town, a collection of small settlements was laid out just north of the mining lease in the area known today as Burra North. The settlements included Aberdeen, laid out by the Scottish Bon Accord Mining Company;

Llwchyrr (pronounced Lew-ish-er), laid out by a smelting company for its Welsh workers; and Redruth, laid out in 1849 by South Australian government surveyors.

It was to Redruth that many Cornish miners flocked. The lots were sold cheaply and the miners were encouraged to build their own cottages on their land. The whole settlement had a very Cornish flavour, with its nostalgic name and its equally Cornish street names — St Day, Truro, St Just, Mevagissey, Lelant, Ludgvan, Illogan, Tregony, Trembath, Morvah, Sancreed, Crowan and Helston. Two other small villages nearby with Cornish names were Copperhouse and Lostwithiel.

From the evidence of contemporary newspapers it is clear that the life style in the early days of Burra was very much influenced by Cornish tradition. Thus the Duke of Cornwall's birthday was observed as a holiday, and it and other special days were generally occasions for competitions in Cornish wrestling. One report in 1848 described how up to 1000 people would gather at Burra to watch the matches. St Piran's day, 5 March, was usually a great Cornish day at Burra and in the early years it was a holiday in honour of their patron saint. The tradition of Midsummer's Eve bonfires was kept for many years, even though the date, 24 June, made it Midwinter's Eve in Burra. Thus it was reported in 1863 that 'it was a red letter day in Cousin Jack's calendar', when juveniles lit numerous bonfires.

Cornish Methodist religion was strongly implanted at Burra from the earliest days. The Bible Christians established themselves for the first time in South Australia when James Blatchford, a miner from Stoke Climsland in Cornwall, found work at the Burra mine. With John Stephens, another Bible Christian from Cornwall, he held prayer meetings in Stephens' house at Redruth. In a short time they attracted other Bible Christians from amongst the miners and the South Australian Mining Association granted land for the erection of a chapel. This was built and financed by the local members and all of this was done before any Bible Christian minister ever reached South Australian soil.

A Primitive Methodist Chapel was opened in Kooringa in 1849 and its local preachers, viz. Messrs Rowe, Symons, Hayes, Berryman, Prior,

Sunday was the day that the Cornish shed their working clothes and dressed up for church. Top hats and frock coats were commonly worn by officials of the mines. This group contains the elders of the Primitive Methodist church at the Redruth section of Burra in about 1875.

Scoble, Moyle and Nicholls, were overwhelmingly Cornish.

Wesleyan Methodist services began in the house of a miner, John Chapman, in 1846 and one year later the South Australian Wesleyan Circuit was divided into three — Adelaide, Willunga (where many Cornish were working in the slate quarries) and the Northern Mines (Burra and Kapunda). At the same time the South Australian Mining Association gave the Wesleyans the lease of an acre of land in Kooringa and the substantial number of Cornish adherents in the town set about building the first chapel. The names of the first leaders amongst the Burra Wesleyans indicate, once again, strong Cornish involvement. They were Messrs Chapman, Moyses, Whitford, Jeffery, Trehair and Bray.

The Burra mine was worked until 1877 and produced £4 800 000 worth of copper. Its early years were its best and it was forced to close for a short period during the Victorian gold rushes. From 1860 onwards it had to take second place to the Wallaroo and Moonta mines. But thousands of people in Australia today can trace their ancestry back to Cornish great-grandparents and great-great-grandparents who were encouraged to come to South Australia by the South Australian Mining Association, who landed at Port Adelaide and who then spent six uncomfortable days travelling by bullock cart to the fabled Monster Mine.

Burra has survived and in recent years it has even seen a small renewal in mining when the Samin company endeavoured to mine some untouched low-grade ore with the aid of modern technology. Something of the Cornish cultural heritage can still be seen in the town, even though nowadays there is no distinguishable Cornish group among the townspeople and farmers of the district. Still standing are some Cornish-built chimneys at the old mine site and close by are the ruins of engine houses built by Cornish stonemasons. Throughout the town the workmanship of the Cornish stonemasons can be noted in many buildings and there are many original miners' cottages still standing, built with their front doors opening on to the footpath.

Paxton Square, a collection of cottages built by the South Australian Mining Association for miners brought out from Cornwall to work at the Burra mines.

Paxton Square, a three-sided complex of cottages built by the Mining Association to house newly-arrived migrants from Cornwall, is still standing and is preserved by the National Trust. Several of the old cottages have been painstakingly restored and are available as holiday accommodation.

Burra was the first large concentration of Cornish in Australia — the first locality where Cornishmen and their families were clustered together in thousands. Strangely, the Burra cemetery has very few headstones that testify to Cornish origins; this reflects the mobility of miners, for they came to Burra mostly as young men with young families. They established a Cornish settlement, but they moved on when times were bad or when gold lured them to Victoria. Most of those that stayed in mining moved on to the copper fields of Wallaroo and Moonta. At the same time many also gave up mining, bought land and became farmers, a tendency that was most pronounced in the years that followed the Victorian gold rushes.

6 The Goldfields Attraction

If the attraction for Cornish migrants in the 1840s was copper, then the attraction of the 1850s was gold. It was discovered first in New South Wales at the Ophir field in 1851, but the centre of activity quickly switched to Victoria where Clunes, Ballarat, Creswick, Castlemaine, Forest Creek, Bendigo and a host of other localities quickly became magnets for tens of thousands of able-bodied 'diggers' looking for fortunes. Between 1851 and 1854 the population of Victoria rose from 76 000 to 220 000, principally because of the 'rushes' to the goldfields, and in 1858 the number of miners in the colony peaked at 150 000. This represented an enormous inflow of men of all nationalities, mostly from overseas but also from the other Australian colonies.

There is no doubt that the Cornish were at the goldfields in large numbers. But they were only part of a restless, heterogeneous army of men moving from spot to spot as each new 'rush' opened up and phased out. The Cousin Jacks scrambled with the Irish, the Welsh, the Scots, Germans, Americans, Italians, French and Chinese in the early years of alluvial mining. The Cornish worked in small parties, often from the same parish in Cornwall, but they seldom formed any concentrated, sizeable group at any locality.

When gold was first discovered in Victoria there were few Cornish miners in the colony. Thus they do not figure prominently in the early years of prospecting. James Flett's *History of Gold Discovery in Victoria* has a detailed list of discoverers of the goldfields and it is noticeable that very few of the names for 1850 and 1851 are Cornish. Thereafter names like Roach and Jewell occasionally appear but Irish, Scottish and English names continue to far outnumber Cornish. There were two notable Cornish successes, however. One was when John Deason found

This well-known illustration of gold diggers working along a stream was the work of J. Skinner Prout (1806–1876) who was born in Plymouth and knew the Cornish countryside across the River Tamar very well. He came to Australia in the 1840s and made many sketches and paintings while roaming throughout New South Wales, Victoria and Tasmania. He later returned to live in England.

a huge mass of gold at Mount Moliagul in 1869 which when melted down and refined of its impurities weighed 2284 ounces (about 65 kilograms) and was sold for £9436. The other success was indicative of the 'clannish' nature of Cornish miners when twenty-two of them claimed to be discoverers of the 'Welcome Nugget' of 2217 ounces found at Ballarat East in 1858.

In South Australia in 1851 the Cornish copper miners were made aware of the gold discoveries when the Adelaide newspapers proclaimed in bold headlines 'Gold in Abundance'. Some left South Australia as soon as the New South Wales finds were made, Captain

Absolom Tonkin of Callington being one. He tried his luck at Ophir but moved quickly to Victoria when diggings became established there.

At Burra the Victorian news was eagerly analysed and sundry miners made ready to visit the diggings. An advance party went in September 1851 and, when most of its members returned in October to collect their families and belongings, it was the signal for a mass exodus from Burra. In December, the South Australian *Register* noted that 100 miners had arrived in Adelaide to join ships bound for Victoria.

A ship journey from Port Adelaide to Port Melbourne or Geelong in 1851 cost £4 and took three to four days; from there it was several days' walk to the diggings. To many miners the fare of £4 was too much, particularly if they wanted to take their families; thus hundreds of them walked overland. One example is provided by the recollections of John Henry Trevena when, seventy-seven years later, his 'Reminiscences of a Journey to the Victorian Diggings' were published in the *Kapunda Herald* on 22 June 1928.

John Trevena was eight years old when he made the journey. His father William, originally from Redruth in Cornwall, worked in the Kapunda copper mine from 1844 to 1852 and it was in the early part of 1852 that the Trevena family — William, Jane and six children — plus three relatives, a fellow-miner and his wife, set off for the goldfields. They had two bullock teams and three horses, one of which John Henry rode most of the way. The horses and the bullocks had to swim across the River Murray while the families were paddled across by Aborigines in canoes. The bullock drays were pulled across the river by Aborigines on the opposite bank.

Trevena recounted the troubles associated with the long drive through the 'ninety-mile desert' (now Coonalpyn Downs), the difficulties of crossing a bridge on the River Loddon which was so rough that the bullocks could not get a footing, and the tedious daily progress that lasted for seven weeks before the party reached Bendigo.

The long trip was worth it for the Trevenas; they found gold quickly in the Bendigo gullies and twelve months later they were back at Kapunda with sufficient money to buy a small farm.

Throughout 1851 and early 1852, the migrants to the Victorian goldfields were, like the Tonkins and the Trevenas, chiefly from the other

Australian colonies. Thereafter their numbers were matched by overseas immigrants who by then had heard the news of the gold discoveries and were catching boats that sailed not only from English ports but from American, New Zealand and South African ports as well.

Most of the overseas immigration entered Victoria through Port Melbourne. William Adams who came from near Launceston, Cornwall, was typical of hundreds who sailed from Plymouth in 1852. His ship, the *St George*, took from 6 October 1852 to 3 January 1853 to reach Melbourne, and then with four friends from Launceston he bought a horse and dray and took five days to reach the Castlemaine diggings. Adams eventually went into business in Castlemaine and stayed to become one of a collection of old people who formed the Castlemaine Pioneers and Old Residents' Association in 1880. Their reminiscences were handwritten in the 1880s in an old ledger and were eventually published in book form in 1972.

The emigration of copper miners from Cornwall to South Australia continued during the gold-rush period, but very few of them stayed in the colony when they landed. As soon as they got off the ship in Port Adelaide they set off to walk to Victoria. Marshall McDermott, the Immigration Officer at Port Adelaide, complained in September 1851 that 'frauds of all kinds are resorted to, to obtain a passage to South Australia in order to proceed to the goldfields'.

In March of 1851 there were more than 1000 men working at the Burra mine. Twelve months later the Victorian exodus had reduced the number to 360 and in November, when the number was less than 100, the lower levels of the mine were allowed to fill with water because there were insufficient hands to operate and maintain the pumps. Kapunda was even worse hit when its mining force was reduced to four men and all work underground ceased.

It wasn't until 1855 that work recommenced in earnest at Burra and Kapunda. By that time fortunes were hard to make at the Victorian diggings and Cornish miners were beginning to drift back to the copper mines. Their return was encouraged by the mining companies who employed agents on the goldfields to recruit capable copper miners at rates of between £8 and £10 a month. Recruitment was stepped up in the early 1860s, when the Wallaroo and Moonta mines were opened.

The Wallaroo proprietors, for example, placed advertisements in Victoria's newspapers stating: 'Miners wanted for the copper mines at Wallaroo. Passage paid'. The Moonta Directors employed S. R. Wakefield as their agent and he recruited several hundred miners with their families soon after the Moonta mines began in 1861.

The movement of Cornish copper miners from South Australia to Victoria was part of one of the biggest internal migrations in Australia's history. Of course they were only part of the total migration of shopkeepers, farmers, labourers, professional people and vagrants, but they were a significant group which South Australia could ill afford to lose. No wonder, then, that they were actively recruited to return and a significant number of them did.

In the history of the early years at the goldfields, the Cornish have been mentioned for their skills at sinking shafts, for their devout Methodism, or for their dislike of the Irish. It was noted, for example, that very few apart from the Cornish could sink and timber a shaft properly, and this was particularly evident when the early alluvial diggings began to be replaced by hard-rock mining, in the mid-1850s.

The Reverend Irving Benson, in his study of Victorian Methodism, noted that there were many Cornish miners 'aflame with the fire of Methodism' at the goldfields. He noted that 'their frank and fearless piety' won them respect amongst the wild and reckless men who abounded at the diggings. On Sundays the sound of the Cornish at their prayers or their hymn singing was heard in many a gully and along the banks of creeks. Companies of miners held classes and prayer meetings in each others' tents and whenever they settled in some permanent community, chapel-building was uppermost in their minds.

Geoffrey Serle, in *The Golden Age*, noted that 'The Methodists were the only denomination to have striking success on the goldfields'. In many places they often 'conducted more services than all the other churches combined' and 'Cornish miners formed [their] nucleus of support'.

A contemporary observer noted that Cornish men and Tipperary Boys (Irishmen) at some of the large diggings used to fight daily. A favourite trick with the skilled Cornish was to sink their shafts quickly and then drive under a neighbouring Irishman's claim. The Tipperary Boy, it was reported, would then suddenly drop through with a yell into the drive of a Cornishman. And woe betide the Cornishman if he was caught!

It was at Bendigo that the Cornish influence was the most noticeable. Diggers who overlanded from Burra formed a concentrated settlement in the western gullies of Bendigo where shaft sinking needed to be a little deeper than usual, but where the potential rewards were greater than in other shallow alluvial areas. At White Hills, Bendigo, the Cornish really showed their competence at hard-rock mining. Here they persisted, when everybody else failed, in an attack on the glistening white conglomerate of the hills. Many previous diggers had blunted their picks on the super-hard rock, but a party of Cornishmen drove through it for twenty-one metres and tapped a fortune in gold in the soft clay that lay beneath.

Amongst the many other Bendigo mines, some were obviously Cornish in their origin and workings. Their names tell the tale; Cornish United, Cornwall and Welsh, Cornwall and Dublin, Duke of Cornwall and Pascoe.

A view across Long Gully towards Sparrowhawk Gully, Bendigo. A former Methodist (now Uniting) church sits on a ridge between the two gullies and was the focal point of the Cornish communities which searched for gold in the two gullies in the 1850s and 1860s.

Sparrowhawk Gully, its extension Long Gully, and one of its adjoining bluffs, St Just's Point, were the focal points of the early Cornish community in Bendigo. And then later, in the 1860s, an adjoining suburb was named Moonta after the South Australian mining town from which many workers came. The whole area was known as 'the singing gullies' because of the habit of the Cornish, with their Welsh counterparts, of singing hymns and carols. On Christmas Day in the Sparrowhawk Gully it became traditional for Cornishmen's Sports to be held, with wrestling, iron quoit throwing, tugs-of-war and foot races.

George Lansell, who became the quartz reef millionaire of Bendigo, made good use of Cornish mine captains. He recruited them often and it was their supervision which did so much for successful mining on the remarkable series of quartz reefs that were opened up in 1862 after the alluvial gold was almost exhausted. Some of Bendigo's shafts were the deepest in Victoria.

Richard Williams was one of Lansell's managers. He was born in Cornwall in 1831 and began work in the mines when he was aged nine. He mined in America for a brief spell and then returned to Cornwall. He came to Bendigo in 1857, worked first on some alluvial fields, and then in the 1860s was employed by Lansell. Later he branched out on his own with the Williams United Mine and made a success of it. He was typically Cornish in that he was an active member of the Wesleyan Church for more than thirty-five years at Bendigo, and he was also somewhat typical in that he had a large family of ten children.

The first religious service conducted in Bendigo was given by James Jeffrey who became a legendary 'stump preacher'. He was born at Illogan in Cornwall and came to Bendigo by way of Burra in South Australia. Later, he returned to South Australia, but this time to Moonta, where he died soon after in 1877.

Jeffrey was described by Blamires and Smith in their *Early Story of the Wesleyan Methodist Church in Victoria*, written in 1886. He was 'a typical Cousin Jack', a short, sturdy man with twinkling eyes. His preaching was a mixture of homely talk, quaint repartee, Cornish brogue, unexpected turns of speech and pertinent illustrations. Amongst the miners he was enormously popular and he was remembered for one of his oft-repeated exhortations: 'Here you diggers, come work out a claim by Mount Calvary'.

At Ballarat there was not the same ethnic clustering amongst the Cornish as there was at Bendigo, but Cornishmen took part in the rebellion of the Eureka Stockade at Ballarat in 1854. They were a small minority outnumbered by the Irish and other ethnic groups; nevertheless, when the rebels were charged by bayonet-wielding redcoats it was noted that the front line of pikemen contained many sturdy Cornishmen who suffered the brunt of the attack. And numerous individual miners of Cornish descent are remembered amongst the successful pioneers of the town. Thus Isaiah Pearce and C. B. Retallack both enjoyed considerable success on the Ballarat mines and built stately homes to which they gave Cornish names, 'Clowance' in Pearce's case, and 'Carn Brea' for the Retallack family's two-storey mansion. Two well-known Cornish managers were William Hicks at the Star of the East Mine and John Trethowan at the British Queen and North Woah Hawp. Two well-known entrepreneurs who began as miners were Josiah Magor and W. Hambly. Magor made a fortune speculating in mining ventures and Ballarat properties before he retired to live in Geelong. Hambly, who had had mining experience in Wisconsin, Iowa and California before coming to the Australian gold rushes, eventually established a very profitable boot-making business in Ballarat.

While the Victorian goldfields overshadowed those in New South Wales, those in the latter State did not completely disappear. Hill End, eighty kilometres north of Bathurst, had several prosperous periods and attracted many Cornish miners. The Alpha Mining Company was formed for reef mining purposes in 1856 and a stamper battery was ordered from Cornwall. Cornishmen were recruited to sink the shafts, to operate the battery and also to construct roasting pits for heating the ore. The roasting pits are still part of the heritage of Hill End, a town that was proclaimed an Historic Site in 1967. The pits were so well constructed that they stand today little changed after more than a century of exposure to the elements and also to thousands of fossicking tourists who regularly visit the old town each year.

The history of thousands of Cornish people in the years after the gold rushes can be broadly divided into three parts. Many stayed on in Victoria and New South Wales and moved into a variety of other occupations. A large number returned to South Australia to Burra, Kapunda, Wallaroo, Moonta and to further copper fields that were opening up in the Flinders Ranges. Some of these also moved into other occupations. A third small group, having had a taste of the goldfields and their pulsating excitement, chose to keep moving on looking for new fields and elusive fortunes.

A structure which is typical of Cornish mining all over the world, this old engine house was built for the Duke of Cornwall mine near Castlemaine, Victoria.

The Cornish who stayed in Victoria can firstly be noted by their descendants. Thus in a simple random search through a Melbourne telephone directory it was noted that there were 11 Tredinnicks, 33 Tregears, 14 Tregenzas, 14 Tregonnings, 51 Trembaths, 27 Faulls and 23 Polglases. All these are common Cornish names that were probably first introduced into the State during the gold rush period.

A good sample of Cornish miners who moved on to bigger and better things is provided in *A Biographical Register of the Victorian Parliament 1859–1900*, compiled by Kathleen Thomson and Geoffrey Serle. Out of 691 entries, some 15 members had Cornish backgrounds, not a large percentage — they were considerably outnumbered by Irish and Scottish members. However, the Cornish link with the gold rush days is often evident. Thus John Dunstan Baragwanath, born in St Ives, worked on various goldfields before becoming a member of the legislative assembly (MLA) in 1856. Thomas Carpenter from St Austell was a mining engineer in the Bendigo area before becoming an MLA in 1859. Frederick Gray, born at Redruth, accompanied his parents to Creswick during the gold rushes and stayed on to open a drapery and grocery business before entering parliament in 1894 while he was in business in Melbourne. John James, from Liskeard, was a miner and blacksmith at Ballarat before becoming an MLA in 1869. Richard Kitto, MLA for Castlemaine in 1869, was a Cornish mine surveyor and manager, and Robert Sergeant, a miner from Callington in Cornwall, was Western Ballarat's MLA in 1859.

Most of the Cornish who worked on the diggings had plenty of experience in mining, but this did not mean that they had a liking for it. In Cornwall it had probably been the only work they could obtain, but in Australia it was usually a first job which might give them enough money to purchase some of the readily available cheap land that their adopted country had to offer. It is a continuing theme in the history of hundreds of Cornishmen in the 1850s and 1860s that they went to the goldfields, enjoyed moderate success, and then bought land with their capital.

Three examples from hundreds of possibilities can be quoted. Benjamin and Eliza Ware arrived in Adelaide from Cornwall in 1850. In 1853, with their sons John and William, they overlanded with a bullock cart to Forest Creek. After little success there they moved to Joyce's Creek, where they made a moderate strike. With their money they bought 186 acres (75 hectares) nearby at a guinea an acre and so began the family farm.

Ellis and Eliza Livock arrived in Adelaide in 1853 and moved directly to the Ballarat goldfields. Here Ellis worked for several years until he had sufficient money to buy land at South Muckleford when it was opened for selection by the Crown.

Henry Trevaskis, born in St Erth, came to Bendigo from Burra in 1852. After some success he purchased land near Heathcote and farmed there for the rest of his life.

There are many examples of South Australians who returned to their own colony laden with gold dust which was immediately used to buy land. Thus the Trevenas have already been mentioned, the Dunstans from Kapunda did the same thing, and in the area between Strathalbyn and Lake Alexandrina, which was being opened for settlement when the diggers were returning to South Australia, there were many Cornish pioneer selectors such as Henry Waters, George Pearce, Henry Pearce, Alfred Varcoe and John Goldsworthy, all of whom had made money at the goldfields.

Amongst the small group which revelled in mining and retained it as a lifetime occupation there is no better example of restless mobility and perpetual gold-seeking than Captain John Treloar who was born at Helston, Cornwall in 1832. In 1849 he sailed for South Australia, and was engaged as an ore dresser at Burra. In 1851 he went to the goldfields and worked with moderate success at a variety of diggings such as Golden Point, Pennyweight Hill, Winter's Flat, Sulky Gully and Buninyong. By then most of the alluvial grounds had been worked out and Treloar joined in the New Zealand gold rush. Here he worked in the South Island for several years and eventually became the manager of a small mine. When this became unprofitable he returned to South Australia and for a short time he was a coach driver in the country areas.

Gold attracted him once again, this time in 1880 with the small rush at Temora, New South Wales. From there he went to Mount Brown in New South Wales and Mount Pleasant in South Australia. When silver and lead and zinc deposits were discovered in the Broken Hill district, Captain Treloar opened a store at Silverton, but sixteen months later he closed it and was off to a gold rush at Teetulpa.

The Teetulpa goldfields had a brief and unprofitable history, so Treloar returned to the Broken Hill area where he was appointed manager of several small but largely unsuccessful mining ventures. Next he was made manager of the Mount Bryan Ranges Mining Association north of Burra, but this was another unsuccessful venture.

In 1893 the Western Australian gold rushes were on and Treloar, by then sixty-one years of age, could not resist yet another chance to make his fortune. For a time he managed the Agnes Mine at Kalgoorlie, but then he made use of his fifty years of mining experience and established himself as a consultant to numerous companies that were operating at Kalgoorlie and Coolgardie. At the same time he purchased and sold several mines, floated a few new gold mining companies and generally saw out his final years as the equivalent of a mining 'adventurer' in his native Cornwall.

Captain Treloar stayed with mining all his life, while others moved out of mining very quickly to become farmers. Edward Dunstan was an example of one Cornishman who tried to do both.

Dunstan was born in the parish of Wendron, Cornwall in 1841. He accompanied his father and brothers to Kapunda in 1847, and then to Castlemaine in 1851 when he was a boy of ten. Here the family had moderate success and Edward stated in his memoirs that 'the gold fever . . . got to me'. He made three trips to the diggings, returning each time to Kapunda where his father had established a farm.

When the Castlemaine diggings were worked out, Dunstan tried farming for a while, but since 'the roaming spirit was still strong' he sought and obtained work at the Blinman copper mine in the Flinders Ranges. From there he moved further north and worked for a brief period at the Yudnamutana copper field, but gave that up to return to work in the mine at Kapunda.

Next he was off to a goldfield at Hokitika in New Zealand, and when this was a failure it was back to Kapunda for a short spell before the Gympie gold rush in Queensland attracted him. His memoirs record that 'he did no good at Gympie' so he went to the Peak Downs Copper Mine for two years and then back to the Kapunda mine for a further year.

In 1871, when Edward was thirty years old, he finally shook off the 'roaming spirit' and he selected land near the town of Jamestown under a government credit purchasing scheme. Here he established a farm for his family, which eventually consisted of eight children by his first wife Anne and four children by his second wife Elizabeth. Edward called his farm 'Wendron' after his birthplace in Cornwall and he died there in 1924.

Another Dunstan family history paid tribute to Cornish women when it told the story of Jane Dunstan, wife of Richard, who arrived in South Australia with seven children in 1849. Jane's life illustrates many of the heartbreaks and hardships that the wives of Cornish miners experienced. The family moved to Burra and soon afterwards their youngest child died. In the meantime Jane had become pregnant for the eighth time. After the birth her husband died and she was left in Burra with her eldest child Richard, then fifteen, as the family's breadwinner. A few months later another child died in an accident and it was soon after that tragedy that Jane decided to take the family to the Victorian goldfields. She booked passage on a waggon and, family legend has it, kept her money in her stays because she did not trust the driver and didn't change her clothes for the entire six weeks of the journey. The family reached Vaughan, near Castlemaine, and were befriended by earlier arrivals from Burra. Jane eventually married one of these friends, Thomas Rodda, and with him she had two more children, but one died at four weeks old.

Jane Dunstan Rodda died at Vaughan in 1886 at the age of seventy-one. Her obituary recorded that she was widely respected and was 'for 53 years a quiet and consistent member of the Wesleyan Church'.

7 The Wallaroo-Moonta Concentration

If the main focus of Cornish activity in the 1840s was at Burra, and in the 1850s was on the Victorian goldfields, then in the 1860s it was on northern Yorke Peninsula in South Australia where three towns grew up, Kadina, Wallaroo and Moonta. Here two shepherds discovered copper ores, one at what became Wallaroo mines in December 1859, and one at what became Moonta mines in 1861.

Not a single outcrop of rock juts above the limestone plains of northern Yorke Peninsula. There are no creeks or gullies, so it is only along the coast that bedrock can be viewed. Here small fragments of green and blue copper carbonate provided the first clues for Walter Watson Hughes, a pastoralist, and it was he who encouraged his shepherds to search for ore bodies.

When mining began, the extent of the lodes had to be proved by digging trenches, or costeens as the Cornish called them, to discover what was beneath the limestone capping of the plains. They proved to be large and rich bodies of ore, and so a mining era began that lasted from 1860 to 1923. The earliest years were the most profitable and thousands of Cornish were attracted to the new mining towns from three main source areas, Burra, Victoria and Cornwall. Each of these areas had passed its peak of mineral production in the 1860s, so the Wallaroo and Moonta discoveries came at a fortunate time.

By now the South Australian Government had introduced mineral leases to repeal the old Mineral Survey purchase system. Portions of the land near each discovery were converted from pastoral leasehold to mineral leasehold in eighty-acre (thirty-hectare) sections. Each mining company asked for and received several leases. The lease agreement was for a term of ninety-nine years with a rent of one shilling per acre and sixpence in the pound on the annual declared profits of mining.

Two companies were formed, the Wallaroo Mining Company and the Moonta Mining Company. The ores from the two mining areas were treated at a large smelter on Wallaroo beach and the Wallaroo company expanded to become the Wallaroo Mining and Smelting Company. Then, in 1890, when both mines had worked out their high-grade ores and were shifting to low-grade ores, the two amalgamated to form the Wallaroo and Moonta Mining and Smelting Company.

The Mining companies had as major shareholders, and therefore usually as directors, a small number of South Australian pastoralists and businessmen who eventually became very wealthy because of the dividends the mines paid. From early in 1860 the directors were seeking good miners and, since the experiences at Kapunda and Burra had already proved the value of the Cornish miner, it was Cornishmen they most actively sought. Hundreds left the declining Burra mines and travelled the distance of 120 kilometres overland on foot, on horseback or in drays, to take up offers of secure and better-paid jobs. As already mentioned, the directors employed agents on the Victorian goldfields, and many a frustrated Cornish miner left his unproductive diggings and accepted a free passage from Melbourne to the new copper fields of South Australia.

The Wallaroo and Moonta directors also followed the example of Henry Ayers with the Burra mine and engaged agents in Cornwall to recruit miners for them. On one occasion, in 1883, the Wallaroo directors sent Captain Richard Piper from Wallaroo to Cornwall to recruit for them. He inserted advertisements in Cornish newspapers which read:

> Wanted immediately, fifty good miners, including steady young men, also married men with their families, to proceed to Wallaroo Copper Mines, South Australia. For rates of wages and all particulars apply at once in person to Mr Richard Piper, 3 Falmouth Road, Redruth.

Piper was very successful. He returned to South Australia with some

Five Cornish miners and two surface workers at the Wallaroo mines in the 1890s.

405 men, women and children, most of whom were settled in what were called 'new chum' cottages at the mines.

In the 1860s the area was covered with mallee scrub. The name Moonta was taken from Moonta-Moonterra, an Aboriginal name for a particular patch of scrub nearby. Within thirty years the mining communities had removed all timber from the landscape for firewood, fencing and building. The level countryside made transportation easier but, in an area of barely adequate rainfall, it did not provide catchment areas for reservoirs or large dams. The lack of fresh water was a great difficulty in the early days of mining. Underground water was plentiful but it was too highly mineralised to be drinkable. The mining company installed several stills and sold water at 'tuppence a bucket' but the supplies were inadequate. Water was also carted from shallow wells sunk in the coastal sandhills and during the occasional heavy shower of rain every attempt was made to collect the water running off roofs. Women and children even collected water from wheel ruts and shallow pools and many miners dug underground tanks to trap the surface flows. The unsatisfactory water supply fostered epidemics of typhoid, especially amongst the children. The rows of small mounds in the Moonta cemetery are a reminder of these early, unhealthy days when the number of deaths reached as many as 110 in a single week.

The initial success of the Wallaroo and Moonta mines was due, firstly, to the wealth of their ores. Moonta, in particular, had lodes near the surface which were very rich and averages of 30 per cent copper in the ore were common. Such high-yielding ore, and also the large number of lodes, allowed the Moonta Mining Company to be floated without any heavy capitalisation. The mines produced good profits as soon as the ore was sold and the Moonta Mining Company used these profits to expand its operations. The profits were so great that the Moonta Mining Company became the first in Australia to pay a million pounds in dividends. However, at depth the lodes declined in richness. By 1908 the average grade had fallen to less than 4 per cent and in 1918 it was 2.2 per cent.

The early success of the mines was also due to favourable world prices for copper. These fluctuated greatly throughout the life of the mines, from a high around £120 in 1918 to less than £40 in the mid-1880s. The long-term average during the sixty-three years of mining was £72. In the early 1860s copper was selling for about £110 and for the first seven years when the mines were becoming established, and they were selling their richest ores, the price was always more than £80 per ton.

In addition to the major Wallaroo and Moonta mines, the area within what has sometimes been called the Copper Triangle of Wallaroo, Kadina and Moonta had numerous other small mines. A local newspaper, the *Yorke's Peninsula Advertiser*, indicated in 1873 that the area contained no fewer than fifty-four separate mines. Many of these were little better than pits in the ground, but some like the Yelta, Paramatta, Kurilla, New Cornwall and Hamley became sizeable

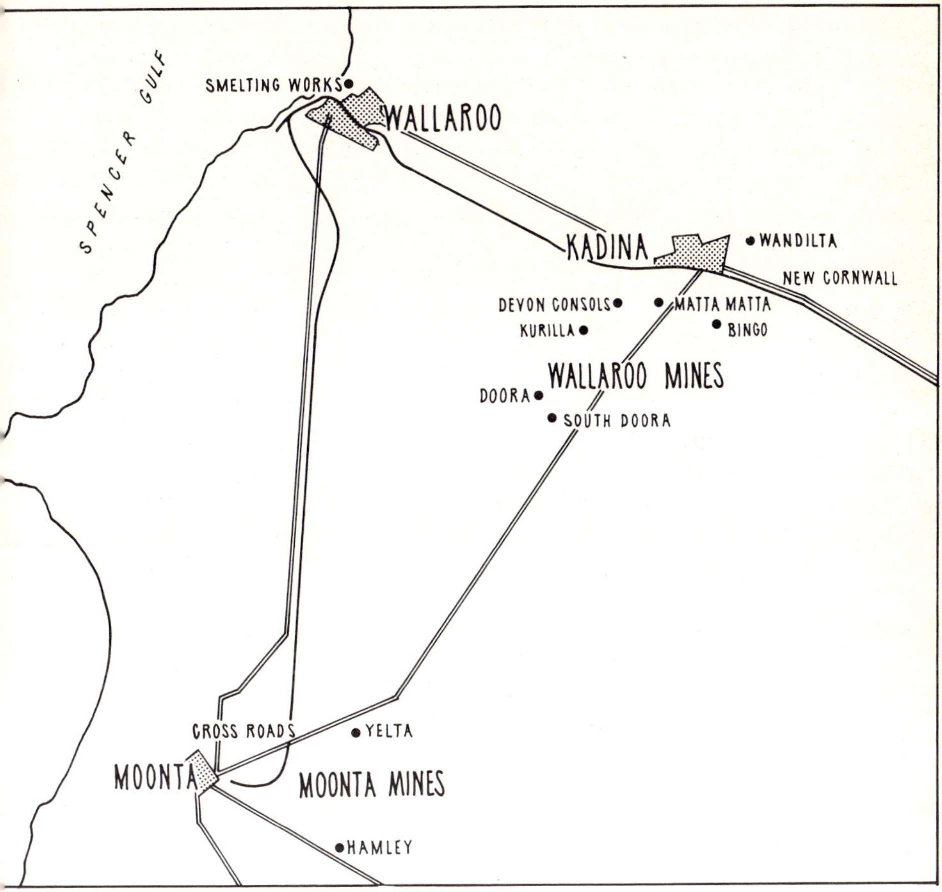

The northern Yorke Peninsula 'Copperopolis' towns and some of the mines in the area.

operations employing fifty to a hundred men.

The Cornish influence in the area undoubtedly had its origins in the recruitment policies of the mine directors and the success of copper mining, but the influence was maintained and fostered by the mining management, who were in the main Cornish. And in this sphere no name was better known and no influence was greater than that of Captain Henry Richard Hancock — yet strangely he was not a native Cornishman. However, Hancock came from a few kilometres across the Tamar in Devon and this was near enough for most Cousin Jacks, particularly as Hancock had obtained much of his mining experience in Cornwall.

Hancock came to South Australia in the 1850s, engaged as an assayer and later as manager at the Wheal Ellen silver lead mine near Strathalbyn. When that mine proved unprofitable, Hancock and most of the other workers from Wheal Ellen proceeded to the Wallaroo and Moonta area. Here, in 1864, the tall, capable Hancock was chosen to replace an unsatisfactory Captain Warmington as chief captain of the Moonta Mines. Later, when the Wallaroo and Moonta companies amalgamated in 1890, Hancock was appointed superintendent of the new company and in 1898, when he retired, he passed his leadership on to his son H. Lipson Hancock, who was superintendent until the mines closed.

Henry Hancock understood Cornish mining customs and he was a devout Wesleyan Methodist. He thus earned the respect of thousands of Cornish miners and, because his mines at Moonta became world-famous, so also did Henry Hancock. Furthermore, Hancock had an interest in mining machinery which led him to foster large and efficient machine shops at Moonta mines. The machine shops produced several notable inventions patented by Hancock; these helped considerably in the later years of the mines when low-grade ores had to be treated by special jigs and crushers before they could be smelted.

Hancock was an autocrat who had complete control of the day-to-day decision making at the mines for more than thirty years. Since he unashamedly favoured Cornish miners and Wesleyan Methodists it is easy to see why Moonta mines, in particular, became such a focal point for Cornishmen in Australia.

Hancock appointed numerous captains — one local newspaper proprietor once described them as being 'as numerous as gooseberries on a bush'. Malachi Deeble, a man of considerable experience first at St Austell, Cornwall, and then at Burra, was his second Captain. Deeble then went farming for a brief period, but when the Wallaroo and

The transfer of building techniques from Cornwall to Australia is well illustrated by these two photographs. At left is the remains of an engine house and chimney, built of local granite, near Camborne in Cornwall. At right is the remains of Hughes's engine house and chimney, built of local limestone, at Moonta Mines.

Moonta mining area was opened up he was lured back to mining to be the captain at Kurilla. When that mine was no longer profitable he was happy to find work as Hancock's deputy.

Other captains who became well-known at Moonta mines were James Barkla, Thomas Cornelius, James Pryor, Nicholas Opie and William Hayes, who were underground men; Joshua Skinner, Christopher Faull and John Dunstan who were surface or 'grass' captains. At Wallaroo mines some well-known captains were Edward Dunstan, who was dismissed in 1869; Harry East; Paul Roach; and

Samuel Higgs, who had a fine reputation and was a special import from Cornwall. Higgs, however, was also dismissed in 1877 and Henry Hancock took over the Wallaroo mines in addition to his responsibilities at Moonta mines.

On some of the smaller mines, well-known captains were John Warren at the Hamley and Paramatta, Thomas Cowling at the Yelta and Wheal Hughes and Thomas Kitto at the Euko.

In the 1860s and 1870s, Moonta Mines was the largest mining community in Australia. In 1872 there were 1300 men working on tutwork, tribute, ore crushing, bagging, handling, on the machines, in the machine shops or in the stores. There were nearly 13 000 people living in the Copper Triangle area or, as a newspaper reporter in the 1870s called it, 'Copperopolis'. Of these, some 6200 people were counted in July 1872 as living within one mile (1.6 kilometres) of Moonta.

It was this area within one mile of Moonta that Oswald Pryor, miner, cartoonist, musician and author, called 'Australia's Little Cornwall', the title of his well-known book. The area included two communities, the government town of Moonta laid out in 1863, and Moonta Mines, a collection of mine shafts, poppet heads, engine houses, churches and scores of miners' cottages.

More than anybody else, Oswald Pryor established the Cornish miner in the consciousness of the Australian people. He was the son of Captain James Pryor from Wendron, Cornwall, and was himself born at Moonta Mines. As he grew up he noted the life style of his father and his fellow-miners from Cornwall. Oswald had the delightful skill of capturing their Cornish eccentricities in cartoon form, dozens of which were published in *The Bulletin.* Later a book of the cartoons was published called *Cornish Pasty: A Selection of Cartoons.* Pryor's name for the area has become so popular that roadside signs outside Moonta now proudly proclaim to travellers that they are entering 'Australia's Little Cornwall'.

Probably the most distinctively Cornish feature of the Copper Triangle in the late nineteenth century was its adherence to

The mechnical shops of Moonta Mines where 134 men were employed in 1890.

A group of tradesmen and apprentices at the mechanical shops in 1890.

Methodism. It was at its height in 1874 when the original single circuit for the Wesleyans (the most numerous of the Methodists) was divided into two circuits, Kadina-Wallaroo and Moonta. The Kadina-Wallaroo circuit had chapels at Kadina, Wallaroo, Wallaroo Mines, Pittenween and Newton. The Moonta circuit had chapels at Moonta, Moonta Mines, Yelta, North Yelta, East Moonta and Cross Roads.

By 1875 the combined total of Wesleyan, Primitive and Bible Christian chapels in the Moonta area was fourteen, three at Moonta Mines, three at East Moonta, three at Yelta, three at Cross Roads, one at North Yelta and two at Moonta. In the Kadina-Wallaroo area there were ten chapels, three at Kadina, three at Wallaroo Mines, three at Wallaroo and one at Pittenween. Thus in 'Copperopolis' there were twenty-four Methodist chapels and they had seating for 9000 people.

The Methodist conferences in Adelaide recognised the importance of the Yorke Peninsula circuits and stationed some of their most distinguished ministers there. Some, like Thomas Ratson and Samuel Knight, also served on the Victorian goldfields and on many occasions they preached to the same Cornish miners in both places.

The Methodist ministers worked with more than fifty local preachers in the Copper Triangle. Together they preached in the style that was familiar in Wesley's Cornwall, plain speaking in a rich emotional style. A typical example was Samuel Knight whose contemporaries described him as 'an emotional preacher'; 'his oration was of the torrential order'; 'his one great aim was the salvation of souls' and 'he was a successful recruiting sergeant in the army of the Lord'. These were the qualities that Cornishmen admired and the Reverend Knight drew large congregations wherever and whenever he preached.

The greatest exponents of emotional religion were the local preachers, and throughout 'Copperopolis' most of these were also officials of the mine. Thus James Pryor, Nicholas Opie and Christopher Faull were forceful Wesleyan local preachers and it is probable that their skills in this regard helped them to become captains of the Moonta mines.

Besides preaching, the ministers and local preachers also administered to other Cornish needs. Thus, amongst the poorly educated

"From Broken 'ill, lad? An' what chapel did 'ee b'long up there?"

One of Oswald Pryor's cartoons about life in Australia's Little Cornwall. The black hat and top coat was typical dress for mine captains.

miners there was a thirst for education, or 'self-improvement' as it was called. The preachers frequently gave lectures on a range of topics designed to improve general knowledge. James Pryor, for example, lectured on mining methods, and visiting ministers who came to the circuits were always called upon to give public lectures. Their subjects varied widely, but a popular one was 'Courtship and Marriage' given by the Reverend John Watsford.

The ministers and local preachers also supported the Band of Hope and the Temperance Union, both organisations designed to educate young people about the evils of drink. Despite this, each of the towns in the area had several hotels and the Cornish reputation for drinking was only slightly dented by numerous appeals for the miners 'to sign the pledge' and give up alcohol.

The finest hours for Cornish Methodism were during their revivals when the ministers and local preachers whipped their congregations into a frenzy of crusading evangelism. One such occurred in 1875 when, at the Moonta Mines Sunday School Anniversary, some of the leading brethren of the church lamented the fact that very few of the young were accepting Christ and that there was very little seriousness of mind amongst the adult congregation. The idea of a revival was suggested and the brethren resolved that it should be strongly investigated.

The Moonta Mines Uniting Church. From 1865 to 1899 it was the Moonta Mines Wesleyan Methodist Chapel and from 1900 to 1977 it was the Moonta Mines Methodist Church.

On 15 March 1875, Hugh Datson, a widely respected church member, was crushed by falling rock in a mine accident. He lingered, critically ill, for a few days but then died from his injuries; this tragic event was the spark that ignited a major revival. On Sunday 21 March, seven people professed to find peace with God at the Moonta Mines church. After that the leading brethren of all the churches organised themselves to encourage as many as possible to come forward to surrender their souls. Prayer meetings were held nightly in all the chapels and the head count of conversions was scrupulously kept; 15 by 4 April, 55 by 11 April, 151 by 18 April, and 304 by 25 April.

Oswald Pryor, in his book *Australia's Little Cornwall*, wrote about the stirring revivals at Moonta. In April of 1875 the Methodists took to the streets in evening processions, with hundreds marching along singing hymns such as *Hold the Fort* and *My God the Spring of All Joys.* Special services were held in all the churches and in many cases the congregation spilled out on to the roadways. The Reverend J. Wright, at Moonta at this time, recorded in a diary:

> Souls saved every night . . . One woman, 60 years of age, while our people were singing 'Come to Jesus' cried out 'Yes I am coming'. She came and fell on her knees, found peace and went on her way rejoicing. How grand to see souls cast themselves on the altar.

Another aspect of Methodism which the miners transposed from Cornwall to Australia was the class meeting. This was held once a week and the class leader, who was also frequently a local preacher, had pastoral care over a group of about a dozen class members. The meetings consisted of Bible readings and also lengthy testimonies to the Christian faith of the members. Henry Hancock attended a class meeting and it is noteworthy that all the Wesleyan class leaders, for example Malachi Deeble, Richard Garland, William Datson, John Wellington and Joseph Jolly, were officers of the mines. In 1868 a report made by a Wesleyan Methodist Minister indicated that Wallaroo had 48 class members, Kadina had 64, Wallaroo Mines had 62, Moonta had 50 and Moonta Mines, clearly the largest community of the faithful, had 180 members.

Moonta Mines was the hub of Australia's Little Cornwall. It was mostly a collection of small miners' cottages built close to the mine shafts. These were very like miners' cottages in Cornwall, but with some modifications to suit local materials and conditions. They were built of local limestone rubble plastered over and whitewashed once a year at Christmas; but some had verandahs as protection from the hot Australian sun and nearly all of them had underground water tanks to collect the rainwater that was so precious in a land of very dry summers.

The miners' cottages were built without regard for any streets, and blocks were fenced off at any angle to include any size and shape. There were no footpaths, no properly made roads and no lights at night. Dotted around were dumps, slimy dams, and open shafts, making it hazardous to venture out at night. Wandering herds of goats and other stray domesticated animals, particularly fowls, added to the general confusion. There were no proper sanitary arrangements and, with rapid increases in the population during times of high copper prices, the settlement became very unhealthy. The Moonta Mining Company eventually had to police the spacing of cottages in the immediate vicinity of some shafts in the face of growing health risks.

The unhealthy nature of much of Moonta Mines, particularly in the area colourfully dubbed 'Cemetery Flat', was responsible for an outbreak of typhoid fever in 1870. Dozens of people died, including Annie Hancock, wife of Captain Hancock, and Sarah Cowling, wife of Captain Thomas Cowling. During the fever period there were many burials in the Moonta cemetery and most of them were carried out in the accepted Cornish manner. In the early days, before the coming of hearses, the coffin was carried by several men, all close relatives, to the cemetery, with the mourners marching behind all lined up in special positions dictated by their relationship with the deceased. Thus near relatives were close to the coffin, and distant friends brought up the rear of the march. There was much singing while on the march and at the graveside. To ''ave a good send-off' was a Cornish ambition and bearers and mourners were usually invited to return to the house afterwards for a lavish spread which was always considered to be part of an appropriate 'send-off'.

Oswald Pryor, with his own love of music, made a special study of the Cornish music at Wallaroo, Kadina and Moonta. He pointed out that, although the modern custom of 'Carols by Candlelight' apparently began in Melbourne in 1938, the Cousin Jacks of Little Cornwall, as far back as 1865, used to sing carols by the light of 'fatjacks' — tallow candles stuck on their miner's helmets with daubs of damp clay. To the Cornish their 'curls' were very precious and Moonta's Johnnie Thomas edited a collection of them and had them printed in Germany in 1893. Thomas organised Moonta carol-singing on Christmas night for decades. Large crowds sat around the rotunda in Victoria Park, Moonta, and listened to a two-hour programme by the combined choirs of the district. A typical Oswald Pryor observation was that the Cornish folk used to like their singing hearty — 'Like 'ee used to be before they music teachers spoilt singin''.

It was in the early decades of the mining at Copperopolis that the Cornish influence was strongest. It stemmed from the emigrants who could still remember the wrestling, the cock-fighting, the Sunday School anniversaries, the tea-meetings on Mondays after important church services on Sundays, and the foot-racing which had all been so popular in Cornwall. They emulated their Cornish pastimes with picnics on special Cornish days and amongst their own generation they kept their customs alive. However the emigrants' Australian-born children, who started to appear in large numbers as teenagers and young adults in the 1880s and 1890s, quickly forgot or abandoned many of the traditions that had been part of their parents' lives and beliefs.

A GRAND WRESTLING MATCH will take place at Christmas, at Burchell's WOMBAT HOTEL, Kadina. 30 10 188

SPORTS FOR THE MILLION.

CHRISTMAS SPORTS AT WHITE LION HOTEL, KADINA.

DURING the HOLIDAYS there will be WRESTLING MATCHES held in both the Irish and Cornish styles, for Prizes named hereafter. Also, HORSE-RACING and other Fun.

20 11 c WILLIAM HANCOCK.

Advertisement from the Wallaroo Times, *27 November 1867.*

The young men and women who were born in Australia, many of them at Moonta Mines, had never seen the revered little chapels of Cornwall where 'heart religion' had been injected into their parents by the likes of Billy Bray. Instead of the disjointed, chapel-sponsored education in reading, writing and large doses of religion that their parents mostly had, the young Australians usually received the benefits of some regular secular schooling. In most families the children were far better educated than their parents and, as they matured, they tended to be critical of many aspects of the old Cornish lifestyle. In particular they found it hard to become involved in the old emotional religion.

The children of the emigrants developed their own interests which were often very different from those of their parents. One notable instance amongst the young men was a love for Australian Rules Football which became very popular in the mining towns.

After ten years of prosperity, the Wallaroo and Moonta mines were only marginally profitable. All the genius of Henry Hancock and his brilliant young engineer Frederick May was needed to find ways to keep the mines viable while the ore grades diminished and world prices fluctuated. The mines suffered greatly from 'the tyranny of distance' which, as Geoffrey Blainey has pointed out, so much influenced the prosperity of Australia. The main copper markets were on the other side of the world and so Moonta and Wallaroo ores had to be rich enough to bear the additional costs of shipping, commission and exchange rates before the ore could be sold.

When copper prices were low the directors cut wages to keep the operations profitable. In early years they were able to do this because the Cornish had very little experience with collective wage bargaining. Accustomed as they were to individuals bargaining for contracts in their work, they were also used to fending for themselves and thus they seldom presented a united front to make demands upon the management. Eventually, however, unionism came to the mining workforce in the form of the Amalgamated Miners' Association (AMA) when a branch was established at Moonta Mines in 1889.

At the end of September 1891, agitators in the union organised a strike for better wages and better working conditions. They thought that the management would capitulate in a few days but, as a few perceptive writers then noted in the newspapers, the strike was doomed to failure from the outset because of its very bad start. The decision to strike was in defiance of the wishes of the Chief Council of the AMA who had been investigating the working conditions of the miners and surface men. And, more critically, the workforce at Wallaroo mines did not adopt 'common cause' with their Moonta counterparts. They continued to work and so did the Wallaroo smelters. Thus the Wallaroo and Moonta Mining and Smelting Company was only partially affected by the strike and it limped along for the rest of 1891 without catastrophic losses.

The men on strike at Moonta suffered great hardships. Throughout October, November, December and January they received only two issues of strike pay at £1 each. Many of them left the district to look for work, but very few were successful. Eventually the strike was broken, early in February 1892, by dozens of men calling at the mines office asking for work. They went back at reduced wages because the world price of copper had fallen during the strike.

This long and disastrous strike was a bitter experience to many of the younger miners and because of it they began to develop an interest in trade unions and political action. Thus when the 'workers' party', the Australian Labor Party, was being organised in the 1890s the miners gave it their support.

Out of this support came John Verran, the first Labor Premier in South Australia. Verran was born in Gwennap in 1856 and was brought to South Australia by his parents when he was less than a year old. He started work at the Kapunda mine as a picky-boy when he was ten years old and a year later he went to Moonta Mines with his family. Here he attended school for a few months before he received a job working underground.

Verran was a Primitive Methodist, a Sunday School teacher and a local preacher. He became President of the Moonta branch of the AMA and when he was forty-four he was elected to parliament. Nine years later, in 1910, he became Premier. He was a man who retained much of the Cornish humour that Oswald Pryor has so well chronicled, and stories about Verran's days in politics are legendary. At the same time he was also capable of sincere religious feelings and once claimed, with tears rolling down his cheeks, that his MP was due to his PM — Primitive Methodism.

8 The Continental Dispersal

In the mid-1860s, Cornish people in Australia were numerous in two areas, the Copper Triangle of northern Yorke Peninsula and the mining areas of Victoria. On Yorke Peninsula, at Wallaroo, Kadina and Moonta, there was the largest concentration of emigrant Cornish families ever found in Australia. In Victoria the Cornish numbers were probably larger than in South Australia but they were dispersed throughout many mining towns, villages and undeveloped diggings. In South Australia the attraction was copper; in Victoria it was gold.

As we have already seen, there was much restless interchange between the two mining areas and also with the small New South Wales copper and gold fields near Bathurst. These areas were to form a kind of launching pad from which many miners moved across the Australian continent to wherever promising new mines were discovered.

The last thirty years of the nineteenth century saw many small-scale internal migrations of miners from their established bases. They migrated in response to economic conditions, either 'pulled' by promises of high wages and potential wealth at rich new copper, gold, tin or silver fields, or they were 'pushed' by low wages and unemployment at the copper fields of South Australia or by similar problems as yields diminished on numerous Victorian and New South Wales goldfields. At the same time emigration from Cornwall continued. It was mainly directed towards the two established mining areas, but it declined in the late 1870s and virtually disappeared after 1886.

There were a few instances when enterprising new mining companies obtained small parties direct from Cornwall, but mostly the directors of new companies sent their agents to South Australia and Victoria to advertise for skilled men to work their new mines.

The continental dispersal of the Cornish miners can be traced chronologically and also in categories according to whether they were copper miners, gold miners, tin miners or silver miners.

After the establishment of the Wallaroo and Moonta copper mines, the next major copper discovery in Australia was made at Peak Downs, 350 kilometres west of Rockhampton in Queensland. A gold prospector, fossicking on the western slopes of the Great Dividing Range in 1861, stumbled across an abrupt pinnacle of copper ore twelve metres high, six metres wide and three metres thick. From the pinnacle a copper lode was traceable on the surface for over 100 metres. Samples of the ore, when sent to Sydney, assayed from between 54 and 77 per cent copper. A Peak Downs Mining Company was formed and by 1864 it was a large-scale mining operation that had built its own copper smelters.

Josiah Dennis, an experienced Cornish miner from Burra in South Australia, was engaged as the chief captain of the mine; another early mine official was Samuel Osborne, also from Burra. In 1867 the company embarked upon an expansion programme and Osborne was employed as an agent to recruit experienced copper miners in South Australia. At the same time the mining town of Copperfield, six kilometres from the established town of Clermont, was officially surveyed and town allotments were put up for sale. The mining company made numerous purchases and constructed rows of cottages for its expected influx of new miners.

Osborne offered miners at Wallaroo and Moonta employment for a minimum of twelve months with a guarantee of at least £3 per week in wages, and skilled tributers could be certain of earning more. Since this was a much better wage than the South Australian mines were paying, there was no shortage of applicants to go to Peak Downs. In January 1868 a party of sixty miners, seven women and twenty-four children was dispatched to the small port of St Lawrence in Queensland. There, in the steamy tropical heat of February, they walked overland for more than 200 kilometres, crossing swollen rivers and high ridges until they reached Peak Downs. They settled at Copperfield and were later joined by other Cousin Jacks from Victoria and several groups brought out by the company direct from Cornwall.

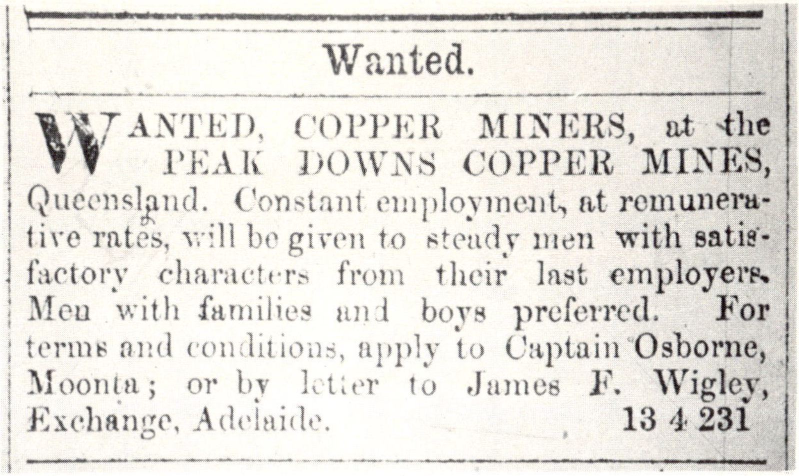

Wanted.

WANTED, COPPER MINERS, at the PEAK DOWNS COPPER MINES, Queensland. Constant employment, at remunerative rates, will be given to steady men with satisfactory characters from their last employers. Men with families and boys preferred. For terms and conditions, apply to Captain Osborne, Moonta; or by letter to James F. Wigley, Exchange, Adelaide. 13 4 231

Advertisement from the Wallaroo Times, *13 April 1867.*

Copperfield quickly became a small town dominated by the Cornish but also with a group of Welsh who were employed to work in the smelters. Two chapels were amongst the first buildings in the town, a Wesleyan for the Cornish and a Congregational for the Welsh.

The Cornish character of the community is well illustrated by the following report in the local newspaper, the *Peak Downs Telegram*, 4 August 1868:

> A fatal accident occurred in one of the shafts at the Copper Mine on Wednesday last when some earth gave way and buried three out of four men who were employed in that part of the mine. The fourth man at once gave the alarm, and the miners quickly removed the earth, when it was found that two out of the three men were comparatively uninjured. The third man, however, had been struck on the breast and killed by a piece of timber which fell with the soil. On the following day an inquiry was held by Captain Lambert, P.M. Several witnesses were examined, and the evidence went to prove that no neglect was

attributable to anyone. On Thursday afternoon the funeral took place. It was attended by a large number of the deceased's fellow-workmen and other residents. He was an Oddfellow, and the procession was proceeded by nearly fifty members of various lodges, the body being carried by hand through the main streets of both townships, while hymns were sung by members of the Wesleyan-Methodist Church, with which the deceased miner was connected. Before starting, a funeral service was held in the Wesleyan Church, and at the grave a second service was held, the Rev. Mr. Parkinson officiating. The deceased was a young man and much respected; he leaves a wife and one child in South Australia. The expense of the funeral was borne by the Company, so that the whole of the lodge money — about £35 — will be at the disposal of the bereaved widow.

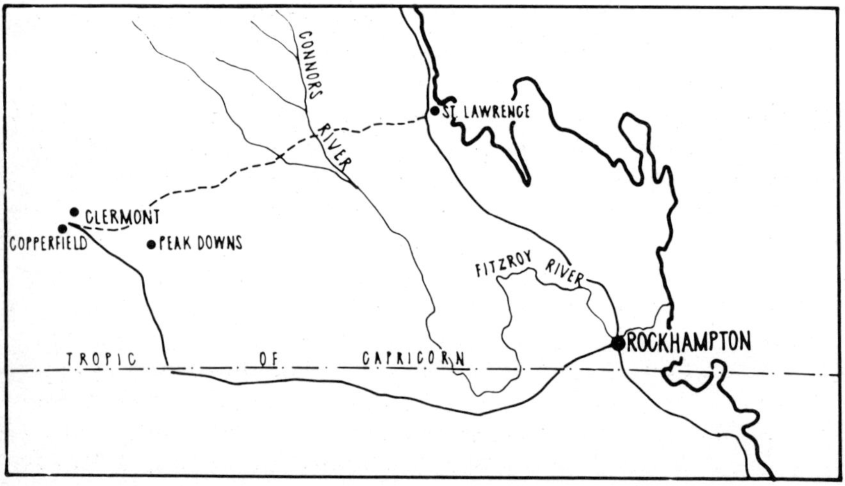

The route to Copperfield, via St Lawrence, in 1868.

The Peak Downs mine was initially very rich and continued to expand and attract Cornish miners until about 1874. Thereafter the ore quality declined and by the end of the 1870s, when world copper prices

Some of the last remaining traces of the Peak Downs mining complex at Copperfield in Queensland. The chimney and the Cornish boiler were part of the smelters which were built during the 1860s.

were spiralling downwards, Copperfield was a ghost town, only a shadow of its former self. Hundreds of Cornish miners left, many to continue their restless roaming across the continent to new mining areas, but many to return to their former homes in South Australia and Victoria.

While the Peak Downs Company was prospering, Ernest Henry discovered the Cloncurry deposit in Queensland in 1867. He named it the Great Australian Mine but found difficulty in attracting a work force to such a dry, hot, remote area. In England, he sought money to help him finance the mine and he also appointed Captain A.S.R. Osborne from Cornwall, a brother of Samuel Osborne, to manage his mine. Osborne and a group of miners sailed to Sydney where he engaged further men to bring his party up to thirty. From there he sailed to Normanton in the Gulf of Carpentaria and on 7 May 1868, with the nucleus of another 'Little Cornwall', Osborne started work at Cloncurry. The venture was not a success, however, and Osborne resigned in 1869. He moved off to manage a small mine at Rosewood, near Rockhampton. Some of his men followed him and others went to Peak Downs. Cloncurry was born again as a copper mining area in the 1880s, but it never again had the same concentration of Cornishmen to excavate its ores.

Wallaroo (1859), Moonta (1861) and Peak Downs (1861) were followed in 1863 by what was thought to be Victoria's opportunity to profit from the prevailing high world prices of copper. This was the discovery of a copper lode on the banks of the Thomson River in Gippsland. The area had been prospected for gold and was not far from the rich gold mine at Walhalla. However, the copper lode was in steep terrain and a succession of syndicates and companies was never able to make a success of it. Several Cornish miners from the goldfields tried their luck with it and one, Ambrose Halifax from Kapunda in South Australia, made a valiant attempt to make it pay. He worked the mine on tribute for the Gippsland Copper Mining Company, but although he was confident that the ore was every bit as good as that found at Burra or Moonta, neither he nor any subsequent group could develop a profitable mine.

In 1869 the Mount Perry copper deposits, 100 kilometres west of Bundaberg in Queensland, were discovered. Captain A.S.R. Osborne was quickly on the scene and he proclaimed that the ores would rival Moonta in its best days and would be superior to either Peak Downs or Cloncurry. There was a short delay while a mining company was organised, but by the end of 1870 Osborne's brother Samuel was acting as an agent once again in Wallaroo and Moonta. His terms were still the same, a twelve-month contract at £3 per week minimum. Throughout 1871 and 1872 Osborne dispatched several hundred copper miners to Mount Perry and several captains were also engaged for some of the small mines near the main deposit. Thus, Captain Tredenick went with a special party of thirty miners to work a small mine and Captain Datson received an appointment as manager of the Boolboonda mine. Other mines, viz. Wheal Damsel, Wheal Haven and New Moonta, had very clear Cornish associations.

At the town of Mount Perry, a large party of miners from South Australia had to be accommodated in a new 'suburb' in 1872. The streets that were planned were appropriately named Moonta Street,

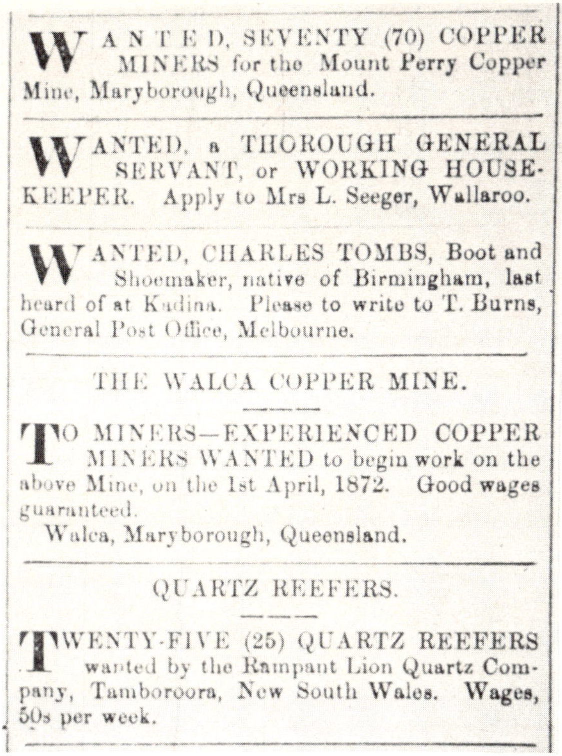

WANTED, SEVENTY (70) COPPER MINERS for the Mount Perry Copper Mine, Maryborough, Queensland.

WANTED, a THOROUGH GENERAL SERVANT, or WORKING HOUSE-KEEPER. Apply to Mrs L. Seeger, Wallaroo.

WANTED, CHARLES TOMBS, Boot and Shoemaker, native of Birmingham, last heard of at Kadina. Please to write to T. Burns, General Post Office, Melbourne.

THE WALCA COPPER MINE.

TO MINERS—EXPERIENCED COPPER MINERS WANTED to begin work on the above Mine, on the 1st April, 1872. Good wages guaranteed.
Walca, Maryborough, Queensland.

QUARTZ REEFERS.

TWENTY-FIVE (25) QUARTZ REEFERS wanted by the Rampant Lion Quartz Company, Tamboroora, New South Wales. Wages, 50s per week.

Advertisement from the Wallaroo Times, *23 March 1872.*

Burra Street, Kooringa Street and Kapunda Street.

Captain Israel Bennett, who was mentioned in Chapter 4, came from Kapunda in 1872 to manage some of the smaller mines. He stayed to become the chief manager in the area, the principal layman and local preacher in the Wesleyan chapel, and chairman of the Perry Shire Council in 1884, 1886 and 1889. J.L. Pearson, another Cornish manager from South Australia, was a later chairman of the Council from 1905 to 1908.

The Mount Perry mines operated until 1913 and maintained close contacts with Wallaroo and Moonta, with many interchanges of men and ideas. Many South Australians returned to their home colony after completing contracts at Mount Perry, but many also stayed on. The local death register indicates some of those who stayed: John Francis, Wesleyan Methodist of New Moonta via Mount Perry, a miner born in Cornwall, who died in 1890; James Trathern, Wesleyan Methodist of Boolboonda Mine, a miner born in Cornwall, who was killed in the shaft in 1893; Joseph James Kelley, Methodist of Mount Perry, a miner born at St Day, Cornwall, who died in 1910.

In 1870 some rocks at Cobar in New South Wales were picked up as interesting samples of coloured stones by two Danish boring contractors. It took a Cornish woman, the wife of a friend, to point out that the pretty stones were copper ore and a copper mine was born.

The first ore from Cobar was taken overland to the River Darling and sent down to South Australia by river steamer to be smelted in Adelaide. The ore was very high grade and a tribute party led by Cornishman John Varcoe went off to develop the mine. At the end of 1871 Captain Lean and a party of miners from Moonta were recruited to begin full-scale production.

Two companies operated in the early 1870s and, in 1876, they combined to form the Great Cobar Mining Company Limited. This became a large and wealthy company that lasted until falling copper prices brought about its closure in 1920. In 1961 mining operations began again and Cobar is once again the principal copper producer in New South Wales.

In 1874 an outback Methodist missionary discovered that Cornishmen had been conducting services in an old store in Cobar. He recommended that the town should become part of the Wesleyan Circuit but it was not until 1879 that the first ministerial appointment was made. A chapel was quickly erected but this was destroyed by fire. A new chapel was built in 1882. It was replaced by a new church in 1914 but the original corrugated-iron chapel still stands and is used as a Sunday school.

In the 1880s and 1890s there were three other major copper deposits discovered and mined in Australia: at Chillagoe in Queensland, at Mount Lyell in Tasmania and at Mount Morgan in the Northern Territory where the copper was located beneath a rich gold deposit.

This prominent building in Cobar, New South Wales, is the former office complex for the Great Cobar Mining Company. It has been restored and is now used as a museum.

However, in these decades there was a noticeable waning of Cornish influence and representation. Cornishmen did work at all of the mines mentioned, but their numbers were small.

It was during the 1840s, 1850s and 1860s that the bulk of the Cornish came to Australia. Most of the arrivals were young men in their late teens or early twenties. By the 1880s they were middle-aged and had lost the taste for roaming Australia in search of new El Dorados. Many of them had given up mining for farming or shopkeeping and very few of them encouraged their children to take on the hard life of mining as a career. At the same time the Cornish captains tended to be ageing and out of touch with mining developments. Most of them had gained their positions because of practical mining experience in Cornwall and

Australia in the 1850s and 1860s. In the 1880s Cornwall was no longer a force in the mining world and its practical experts were being replaced by mining engineers and metallurgists from America. These brash young men relied more upon sophisticated engineering and scientific principles than simple hard-rock mining to produce profits.

Chillagoe, 220 kilometres west of Cairns, undoubtedly attracted many of the Cornish when copper ores were discovered in 1888. In a vast and diverse area that was mined until as late as 1943, silver, lead and tin deposits were also found. The name of Penzance mine, one of many, betrays the presence of the Cornish; Captain James Pryor from Moonta Mines was sent by his directors in 1891 to inspect the Chillagoe mines. An offer had been made to the directors for the purchase of a substantial number of shares, but Captain Pryor's report was not favourable and the directors did not buy.

Many Cornish were attracted to the gold rushes of Gympie (1867), Charters Towers (1872) and Coolgardie (1892). But here again, just as on the Victorian goldfields, the Cornish were a minority absorbed into a heterogeneous mass of 'diggers' from all parts of the world. After the initial finds in shallow diggings, many of them stayed on in the towns that grew up and took jobs with the reef mining companies which sank deep shafts on the quartz lodes.

The Coolgardie field, and Western Australian goldfields generally, were opened during periods of low copper prices (below £50 per ton and falling) and much unemployment at Wallaroo and Moonta. Hence they attracted many Cornishmen from South Australia and middle-aged Cousin Jacks went to the goldfields with their younger counterparts who had been born at Burra, Wallaroo or Moonta.

A correspondent in the *Peoples Weekly*, the Moonta paper, wrote from Western Australia in 1895 urging his friends to come to the goldfields because 'you miserable ill-paid Moonta miners [have] a chance to earn a decent livelihood'. Those that made the long trip often stayed for a short time in 'Moonta Camp' at Boulder, a tent community which was a kind of half-way house until regular employment could be obtained on any of the numerous mines. And at such mines, particularly the smaller ones which the new scientific managers chose to overlook, old Cornish captains were often in charge. Thus W. Rowe from Moonta was captain at the Maritana and Napier claims, and Captain Charles Truscott from Kadina managed the Faith mine. Captain East, Captain Nankivell, Captain Francis, Captain Beaglehole and Captain F. Rodda were all from Yorke Peninsula and all had managerial positions on the Western Australian gold mines.

One of the great Cornish captains in Western Australia, in that he was able to match any of the new managers from America (including Herbert Hoover, later to become an American President), was Captain William Oates who was born at St Just-in-Penwith in 1842. Oates did not emigrate until 1884 and then he was brought out to Bendigo as one of George Lansell's managers.

Oates was at the Western Australian goldfields early and he was soon appointed as a consulting engineer to several of the big mining companies. In 1894 he was elected Mayor of Southern Cross and in 1897 he entered the Western Australian parliament as a Labor member after receiving solid voting support in the goldfields electorate.

There were several other notable Cornish people on the goldfields and the Cornish-South Australian influence was a factor in the rise of the Western Australian Labor Party. They were noted also for their Cornish carols at Christmas time and they figured prominently in the Boulder Choral Society, the Boulder Mines Band and the Amalgamated Miners' Association Band. Cornish wrestling was a popular pastime and South Australian Methodist ministers, who were required to serve in the Western Australian circuits, found good congregations of Cousin Jacks in small chapels at Southern Cross, Coolgardie, Kalgoorlie, Boulder and further afield in places like Kanowna, Menzies and Leonora.

Another metal familiar to Cornish miners, tin, was discovered in the New England highlands of New South Wales and across the border at Stanthorpe in Queensland, at about the same time as copper was found at Mount Perry and Cobar, in the early 1870s. At Elsmore, Inverell, Tingha, Vegetable Creek (later Emmaville), Tent Hill and other localities, hundreds of miners worked on twenty-acre (eight-hectare) leases that contained alluvial tin. There were many Cousin Jacks among them and names such as Captain Pascoe, Wheal Johnson and Wheal Edith clearly indicated the Cornish presence at Stanthorpe in 1872.

Because the black tin ore was plentiful and of high grade initially, it helped Australia to be the largest producer of tin in the world, from 1873 to 1882. However, by the end of the century, the alluvial tin had been almost exhausted and only one hard-rock mine on a tin lode was having any success. The few Cornish tinners who lingered long enough to see the ores begin to disappear left the last pickings to numerous Chinese and moved off to either Herberton in North Queensland or Mount Bischoff in Tasmania. There the deposits lasted longer, but no large Cornish concentrations were responsible for the mining development.

Throughout the first half of the 1880s the world price of copper dropped, from £60 to £38 per ton. This brought much distress to the copper fields of Yorke Peninsula, where it was usually considered that a price of £58 per ton was needed to keep the mines at full employment. Fortunately, throughout these years unemployment for hundreds of the miners was avoided by migration to the Barrier Ranges where firstly Silverton and then more spectacularly Broken Hill were opened up as major mining areas. Thus the economic conditions of the times 'pushed' a large slice of Australia's Little Cornwall to the new silver, lead and zinc mines across the South Australian border into New South Wales.

At Silverton in 1882 and 1883 a town was formed and 'Silverton News' became a regular feature in the Wallaroo and Moonta newspapers. Details indicated that Cornish men were working the Umberumberka Extended mine under Captain Phillips and the West Umberumberka was being supervised by Captain Williams.

In 1883 Charles Rasp discovered the Broken Hill mining field and one of the little-known pieces of history is that on the day of his discovery he was working with two companions, one of whom was John Poole, a Cornishman who had worked at Kapunda. Poole was one of the original owners of Broken Hill shares, but he sold them within a year of getting them and well before they reached any great value.

It wasn't until late in 1884 that mining began in earnest at Broken Hill and a Cousin Jack named Rosewarne was the first to begin sinking a shaft that was appropriately called Rasp's shaft.

In 1885 an exodus from Wallaroo and Moonta was noticeable and although the local newspapers debated the wisdom of tackling the long journey to the Barrier through dry country, and discussed the likelihood of catching lead poisoning, it was undeniable that work was available at Broken Hill and often it wasn't at Wallaroo and Moonta.

The *Yorke's Peninsula Advertiser* published many paragraphs of 'Barrier News' throughout the 1880s because so many of its Moonta patrons had relatives at Broken Hill. The paper reported that Captain George Rogers, a man known for his experience at Moonta, was manager of the Junction Mine; that Captain Mathews was opening up the Round Hill mine, and that Captain Richard Piper, formerly of Wallaroo Mines, had been appointed the underground captain at the Broken Hill Proprietary mine.

Captain John Warren from the Hamley and Paramatta mines at Moonta became a very successful manager of the Block 10 Mine at Broken Hill, and another successful captain at the South and Central Mines was William Morish.

Morish was born in Truro, Cornwall, in 1844. In the early 1860s he worked at Wallaroo Mines and from there he went to Bendigo, Ballarat and Cobar where he was an underground captain. He moved to Broken Hill in 1886, made a success of his job as captain, and also speculated successfully in Barrier mining shares, making enough to be able to retire in Adelaide with a small fortune. He was a typical Cousin Jack miner in that he moved from place to place amongst the mining fields of Australia, but he was atypical in that he invested heavily in shares. This was not a common Cornish characteristic and lists of shareholders for major mining companies can be searched in vain for any strong indication of Cornish involvement.

Piper, Warren and Morish were in the minority amongst the big mine managers at Broken Hill: they tended to be American mining engineers or at least men with American rather than Cornish experience. At the lower levels of management, however, there was still a need for the practical Cornish captains, mainly because they could be hired at a fraction of the salary of a mining engineer. Thus many practical miners who had learnt their skills in Cornwall and honed them at Wallaroo, Moonta or Burra were elevated to become captains at numerous small, and eventually unsuccessful, prospects in the Broken Hill area. Captain T. Tregoweth ran the Rise and Shine mine, Captain T. Rowe managed the Hidden Secret, Captain Tresize had the Bonanza, Captain Penberthy the Big Hill, Captain Dunstan the Anaconda, Captain Hawke the Lady Bevys, Captain Stevens the New Mile, Captain Bennett the Rockwell Paddock, Captain Eddy the Eaglehawk, Captain Hicks the Great Britain and Captain Ellis the War Dance.

As Geoffrey Blainey pointed out in *The Rush that Never Ended*, Broken Hill was never a Cornish mining town in the way that Moonta or Burra was. It developed in a different era, when the migrations from Cornwall were waning and the mining population which grew up around the first shafts was derived from all over Australia, indeed all over the world, when the richness of the deposits became known. Nevertheless, the Cornish element was significant in the first twenty years at Broken Hill and it showed in many ways.

In 1892 a Cornish Association of Broken Hill was formed and John Dunstan, formerly of Burra, was its first president. Its aims were to foster the mutual pleasure and profit of the Cornish community. Many Cornish lived in a south Broken Hill suburb called Moonta Town and many patronised the Duke of Cornwall Hotel. Cornish Methodism was strong as soon as mining began. The first religious service at Broken Hill was given by George Paynter, a Bible Christian from Camborne and South Australia. In 1886, at a Methodist church anniversary, it was noted that the choir was composed chiefly of Moontaites. In 1887 Jacob Burrow, a Cornish wrestling champion, established the Blende Street Primitive Methodist Chapel; he was reported to be a very effective local preacher to the Cornish miners.

All three Methodist groups, the Bible Christians, the Primitive Methodists and the Wesleyans, had thriving chapels by the end of the 1880s. Their ministers were appointed from South Australia and many of them came after experience at Wallaroo, Moonta or Burra.

As the nineteenth century drew to a close, there were hundreds of Cornishmen throughout Australia who could look back upon forty or fifty years spent at places scattered across the Australian continent and even, in some cases, New Zealand. Settled as many of them were on family farms, or retired in a large town or capital city, they still spoke with a Cornish brogue when they recounted their adventures at places like Burra, Bendigo, Peak Downs, Gympie, Charters Towers, Moonta, Broken Hill or Kalgoorlie. One of the retired, Henry Richard Hancock, spoke highly of them all when he was reported in the *Peoples Weekly* thus:

> Since [Captain Hancock] left Moonta he had visited many mining centres in Australasia, and in each place he had found miners from Moonta and Wallaroo Mines. He had heard a great deal about them from those in authority over them, but in no single instance had he ever heard one word against them in their capacity as miners, but on the other hand he had heard a great deal in their favour. In Kalgoorlie and other places in the West they were in the front rank as miners, while at Broken Hill they were not a whit behind. Even in far-off New Zealand he heard good concerning them.

9 The Non-Mining Immigrants

Most of this book has concentrated upon Cornish miners, for they were numerically the most significant group to emigrate from Cornwall. Because of their special occupational skills, they are also easy to distinguish as contributors to the development of Australia. But it must not be forgotten that there were other Cornish people who came to Australia. They did not come in large close-knit groups, and they never achieved the same geographical concentrations that the miners did, but nevertheless they came, they became integrated with the Australian way of life, and some of them made significant contributions to the evolution of our society.

The non-mining immigrants differed from the miners in several ways. They were never as mobile as the miners, they came from a range of social classes and not a single class, they had a variety of occupations, and many of them came as paying passengers rather than as assisted immigrants.

In an attempt to focus on non-mining immigrants and to make some assessment of their contributions, a study was made of all the Cornish non-miners who were considered sufficiently worthy to be given a biography in two standard Australian reference works. The first of these is the *Australian Dictionary of Biography* published by Melbourne University Press. The first six volumes cover the periods 1788–1850 and 1851–1890: the placing of a name in these periods is determined by 'when he/she did his/her most important work' and therefore the periods would appear to be appropriate when looking for original immigrants from Cornwall.

The other reference work is the *Dictionary of Australian Biography* by Percival Serle, first published by Angus and Robertson in 1949.

In nearly all cases a person's biography indicates his or her place of birth and this was the means used to isolate the Cornish people. They were very few. For example, Serle's work has 1030 entries, of whom approximately 484 were born in the English counties. Of these, fewer than ten were born in Cornwall. This figure contrasts with approximately 124 entries for Scots and eighty-two entries for Irish. The number of Cornish in the six volumes of the *Australian Dictionary of Biography* was also small and altogether from both sources only thirty-seven non-mining Cornish-born people could be found. It is clear then, that these emigrants were not a dominating influence in Australia. However, amongst this special group of thirty-seven there were numerous people of quality.

The group can be subdivided into classes or sub-groups that reflect the subdivisions that are recognised in the history of Australian society. Thus, in the beginning there were the convicts and some of the group distinguished themselves in this company.

John Arscott was a carpenter in Truro, Cornwall, but was transported as a convict to Australia in the First Fleet. From Port Jackson he was transferred to Norfolk Island where he distinguished himself by saving the wreck of a ship from destruction by fire. He was highly praised for this act and, in 1791, was pardoned.

Mary Bryant (née Braund) from Fowey, Cornwall, was transported for seven years after being convicted of assault and robbery. She married William Bryant, a Cornish fisherman, in Sydney in 1788. With her husband and seven other convicts, Mary stole the governor's cutter and sailed to Timor in an epic voyage of sixty-nine days. The whole party was eventually arrested in Timor. Some of them died in captivity and the rest were taken back to England where they were given new sentences. The newspapers of the day took up their story and Mary Bryant was eventually pardoned soon after completing her original seven-year sentence.

James Ruse from Launceston, Cornwall was transported for burglary. After his sentence expired he took up farming and was granted a title to land at Parramatta. He was the first emancipist to farm successfully, but in later life he had several farms and never achieved any notable success with any of them.

Eight of the thirty-seven were clergymen, of whom six supported the Methodist Church, one the Church of England and one the Congregational Church. The Anglican minister, Philip Palmer, was born at Landrake, Cornwall. He went to Trinity College, Cambridge, obtaining his MA in 1833, and took up an appointment in the Anglican Church at Hobart soon afterwards. He was responsible for the building of Holy Trinity Church in Hobart and he also established three Church of England schools in Hobart.

The Congregational minister, John Gribble, was born in Redruth but came to Victoria with his family when he was twelve months old. He grew up in Victoria, entered the ministry, and spent a lifetime offering help to Aborigines. He opened and supervised missions in New South Wales, Queensland and Western Australia and he published several books about his experiences. His tombstone in the Waverley cemetery in New South Wales describes him as the 'Blackfellows' Friend'.

The six Methodist Ministers were all Wesleyans: Benjamin Carvosso who worked in New South Wales and Tasmania; Francis Tuckfield in Victoria; John Symons in South Australia and Victoria; William Kelynack in New South Wales; Henry Bath in South Australia, Victoria and Tasmania; and William Lawry in New South Wales.

Tuckfield is remembered for his work on Buntingdale Mission Station near Birregurra, Victoria. He established the mission for Aborigines in the late 1830s but, through no fault of his own, the licence for the land was revoked by the government in 1850. Tuckfield then served in several churches in Victoria and died in Portland in 1865.

The early preaching career of John Symons was with miners at Kapunda and on the Victorian goldfields. Thereafter he made a name for himself in Wesleyan church administration and publishing.

Henry Bath also made a name for himself in church administration but at the same time he was described as the 'prince of preachers' and was widely in demand throughout three colonies. William Kelynack had similar talents but his were confined to New South Wales.

Walter Lawry was more a missionary than a Wesleyan minister. After opening the first Methodist church at Parramatta in 1821, he was sent to Tonga. Later in life, after a visit home to England and work in New Zealand, he returned to Parramatta, where he died in 1859. He was buried in a Wesleyan cemetery which has since become known as the Walter Lawry Methodist Memorial Park.

In the broadly 'professional' occupations there were seven members of the group of Cornishmen: two architects, two judges, two journalists, one merchant-turned-politician, and one magistrate.

The two architects contributed greatly to the design and construction of many buildings in Sydney and Melbourne. Thomas Rowe, born in Penzance where he trained as a draughtsman, practised as an architect in Sydney from 1857 to 1895. Some of his best-known buildings were the Sydney Hospital in Macquarie Street; Newington College, Stanmore; Sydney Arcade and Vickery's Building, Pitt Street; and the Presbyterian Church at Ballarat. He also designed many Methodist churches in New South Wales.

Joseph Reed, born in the Parish of Constantine, Cornwall, dominated the architecture profession in Melbourne in the second half of the nineteenth century. He arrived in Melbourne in 1853 and, in 1854, he won a competition to design the Public Library. Some of the other buildings that he designed in a distinguished career were the Exhibition Building, Wilson Hall, Geelong Town Hall, and the Scots, Wesley and Independent city churches in Melbourne.

Scots, Independent and Wesley churches in Melbourne, all designed by the Cornish architect John Reed.

The two judges were Sir James Penn Boucaut and John Laskey Woolcock. Boucaut, born in Mylor, Cornwall, emigrated to South Australia with his family in 1846. He was admitted to the Bar in 1855 and spent many years in politics, eventually becoming Premier of the State. Later he became a Supreme Court judge and was knighted in 1898. Woolcock was born in Truro, Cornwall, and accompanied his father, a Bible Christian minister, to Queensland in 1866. Here he studied for the Bar, had a brilliant career and eventually rose to be a Supreme Court judge in Queensland.

The two journalists were both prominent in New South Wales. Samuel Bennett, who was born in Camborne, came to Sydney to work as a printer for the *Sydney Herald* in 1841. Later he turned to newspaper publishing and was responsible for the *Empire*, the *Evening News* and the *Australian Town and Country Journal*. John Gale turned to newspaper publishing also, but came to Sydney originally as a Wesleyan minister in 1854. In 1857 he started a newspaper in Queanbeyan and later he published the Braidwood *Independent*, the Gunning *Leader*, the Manley *Spectator* and the Junee *Democrat*.

George Marsden Waterhouse was the merchant who turned to politics. He was born in Penzance but began his working life in Adelaide in 1843. In 1851 he entered the Legislative Council in South Australia and in the years 1861 to 1863 he was Premier of the colony. In 1869 he migrated to New Zealand and was Premier of that country in 1872 and 1873.

The magistrate in the group, John Price, son of Sir Rose Price in Cornwall, was also a colourful commandant of convicts. Price was farming in Tasmania in the 1830s but he was made an assistant stipendiary magistrate soon after he married the ward of Sir John Franklin. Next he was made Commandant of Norfolk Island penal settlement and here he earned a reputation for cruel and harsh punishment. In 1854 he was appointed Inspector-General of penal settlements in Victoria and, in 1857, he was beaten to death by convicts at Williamstown, while he was listening to their grievances. Seven convicts were hanged for the crime. In the book *For the Term of his Natural Life* by Marcus Clarke, the character Maurice Frere is based upon published descriptions of Price while he was the Commandant at Norfolk Island.

Although many thousands of Cornish people took up land for pastoral and agricultural pursuits, only five have been noted in the biographies that were examined. One, William Tom of 'Springfield' farm near Cornish Settlement in New South Wales, has already been mentioned (in Chapter 4) because of his association with the discovery of gold.

Alexander Dennis came from a prosperous farming family in Penzance. With his wife, his daughter and two brothers he arrived at Port Phillip in 1840. They took up large sheep runs in Western Victoria and Alexander settled permanently on the Birregurra run which he called Tarndwarncoort. He became a prominent citizen of Colac and was a staunch supporter of the Wesleyan church in the town and district. The Dangars from St Neot, Cornwall, were a pastoral family who took up enormous tracts of land in New South Wales. Henry Dangar had an active life as a successful pastoralist and passed on his extensive landholdings, including Neotsfield on the Hunter River, to his five sons who operated very successfully as Dangar Brothers. They were one of the very few Cornish families who were part of the 'squattocracy' which built up great wealth from sheep breeding in New South Wales. In some of their ventures they were joined by Jeremiah Rundle, also of Cornish birth. Rundle, however, was a squatter in his own right and held considerable land in the Gwydir district, and in the Liverpool Plains and Blight districts of New South Wales. He also had land in the Warrego and Darling Downs districts of Queensland.

John Smith from St Keverne, Cornwall, was another successful pastoralist. He married a daughter of William Tom and acquired land at Molong in New South Wales. Here he established the famous Gamboola sheep stud. At different times he had vast runs on the watersheds of the Lachlan and Macquarie Rivers and these were managed by his sons.

Three Cornish-born engineers are mentioned in the biographies although, one, Sir John Coode, never lived for any length of time in Australia. He was born in Bodmin, Cornwall, and grew up to become the most distinguished harbour engineer in the nineteenth century. From 1878 onwards he made several visits to Australia as a consulting engineer who advised on harbour works in Victoria, New South Wales,

Queensland, South Australia and Victoria. His recommendations led to the establishment of the modern port of Melbourne, and the building of Outer Harbour in South Australia. Modifications he proposed were put into practice at dozens of small ports including Portland, Warrnambool, Lakes Entrance, Geelong, Port Fairy, Lake Macquarie, Mackay, Townsville and Geraldton.

James Martin from Foundry in Cornwall came to South Australia in 1847 seeking relief from asthma. He established a large machinery works in Gawler and produced agricultural implements, mining machinery and railway rolling stock. Martin became Gawler's most prominent citizen. He represented the district in politics in 1865–1868 and again in 1885–1899. One of his partners in the 1870s was Frederick May, from Perranzabuloe, Cornwall, who at twenty-three had been superintending engineer at Moonta mines. May eventually left Martin's employ and started his own business in Gawler with his brother Alfred. They built agricultural implements but specialised in mining machinery for which there was a great demand in the 1880s and 1890s at Broken Hill and the Western Australian goldfields.

Several other non-mining Cornish people who do not fit into neat categories are mentioned in the biographies. John Permewan from Penzance was the principal partner in the firm of Permewan, Wright and Company. They provided carrying services by river and road throughout Victoria and New South Wales. In 1888 they had forty-eight branches in the two States and agencies at almost every railway station. Joseph Wearne, from St Levan, was a successful flour miller in Sydney, operating the Anchor Mill at Bathurst Street. He was also a respected politician in the New South Wales parliament but resigned when he became bankrupt in 1875 after foolish speculation with mining shares. Edward Tregurtha, from Newlyn, operated a successful shipping line between Tasmania and the mainland in the 1830s. He transported sheep and cattle to ports in South Australia and to Hobson's Bay and Geelong. He retired from the sea in 1839, but worked as a shipping agent and tug master at Launceston, Tasmania, for the rest of his life.

Edmund Webb was another Cornishman to marry a daughter of William Tom. He became a very successful storekeeper at Bathurst, was

This statue was erected in Gawler to honour James Martin, the town's most prominent engineer and owner of the Phoenix Foundry. Martin came from Foundry in Cornwall.

a dedicated Wesleyan Methodist and was a member of the New South Wales Legislative Council.

John Lorenzo Young was the only Cornish-born school teacher to be given a biography. He arrived in Adelaide in 1850 and became an assistant teacher at the South Australian High School. Later he established a private school with six pupils; it grew in the 1870s into a school of several hundred boarders and day boys. In premises at Young Street, Parkside, it became the largest independent school in South Australia, but closed in 1880 when Young retired.

William Crocker Cornish from Cornwall was a very successful builder in Victoria after emigrating in 1852. His first contract was the Melbourne Post Office in 1853 and in 1856 he built the Victorian Houses of Parliament. In 1857 he built the Castlemaine gaol and a large part of the Melbourne gaol. In 1858 he built the Bank of New South Wales in Melbourne and in that year he started the major work of his career: in partnership with J.V.A. Bruce he employed 6000 men to build the first thirteen sections of the Melbourne-to-the Murray railway line. He died in 1859 before the project was completed.

No accolade to the non-mining Cornish would be complete without mention of the third and fourth governors of New South Wales. Philip Gidley King originally came with the First Fleet as a member of Captain Arthur Phillip's staff. King became Governor in 1800 and one of his acts was to change the name of Patersonia in Tasmania to Launceston, which was his birthplace in Cornwall. King was succeeded by William Bligh of the *Bounty* mutiny fame. He came from a family that grew up in St Tudy in Cornwall.

This examination of 'notables' amongst the non-mining Cornish has tried to present a fair sample based upon two respected sources. Inevitably some well-known people were missed and each source acknowledges that this would happen. Two that probably deserve a mention are Sir John Langdon Bonython, the newspaper proprietor in South Australia, and Sir John Quick, the lawyer, politician and author from Bendigo who helped frame the Australian Constitution.

It is understandable that very few of the emigrant working-class Cornish were able to improve their status dramatically in one lifetime. There is no doubt that most of them worked very hard and most of them knew that they were better off in Australia than they could have been in Cornwall. They were able to establish a home and had good prospects of obtaining employment, and many of them bought land. Thus they laid foundations for their ancestors, and tens of thousands of those ancestors live in Australia today where many contribute greatly to the good standard of living the country enjoys.

10 The Assimilated Legacy

This book has recognised as ethnic a nineteenth-century group of Cornish people who emigrated to Australia mostly in the years 1840 to 1880. It is the purpose of this chapter to discuss the question: what did this group leave as a legacy that can be identified in the Australian landscape and in Australian society?

Any examination of Australian maps will show that the Cornish have left their mark in numerous place names. Thus it has already been indicated that Governor Philip King of New South Wales was responsible for naming Launceston after his birthplace in Cornwall and this is only one example of a practice which was responsible for names such as Truro and St Ives appearing on Australian maps. The gazetteer for the Australian series of 1:250 000 map sheets indicates that there are four Truros in Australia and also a Truro Creek. There are two Launcestons (the less well-known one being in Queensland), three St Ives, two localities called Penzance, a Camborn and four Trelawnys. In South Australia nine small (unworked) mines are officially recorded with the prefix Wheal, and throughout the continent the descriptive 'Cornish' has been applied many times, for example, at Cornish Bore (SA), Cornish Creek (Qld), Cornish Jimmie Creek (Qld), Cornish Point (NSW), Cornish Well (SA), Cornish Well Creek (SA), and Cornish Mount (WA).

Across the Australian continent, the ruins of hundreds of small mines can be found in the landscape. And here again the descriptive 'Cornish' is frequently used, this time by local people who can recall that it was Cornishmen who worked the mine. Thus they speak of old 'Cornish' boilers lying abandoned in the scrub and the tall circular smoke-stacks of old mines are invariably referred to as 'Cornish' chimneys. At Burra, in South Australia, local guides will point out the tall circular chimneys built by the Cornish and at the same time they will indicate the square-set chimneys that were the trademark of Welsh builders.

From Chillagoe to Mount Lyell, from Bathurst to Northampton, there are still unmistakable signs of the Cornish mining occupancy. In many cases the old mines have almost been obliterated from the landscape and only the most ardent adventurers can today find traces of their nineteenth-century buildings. But in other cases third- and fourth-generation descendants of the original miners have restored some of the buildings their ancestors created and nostalgic tours are available for those who wish to recapture the romance of the mining days. In Charters Towers, for instance, the once thriving stock exchange building is now a mining museum. The old gaol at Silverton, the former general offices of the Great Cobar Mining Company, and the old home of a prominent mine captain at Northampton are also open to the public now as museums. In each of these, and in many other museums, there are indications of the mining heritage brought to Australia by thousands of Cornish folk.

Fittingly, it is at Australia's Little Cornwall, Moonta and Moonta Mines, that the most striking remnants of Cornish occupancy can be found today. And yet it is fast disappearing; miners' cottages which stood five years ago are tumbling in ruins, and signposts thoughtfully placed by the Moonta Branch of the National Trust of South Australia are the only indicators of where stood old buildings such as the mines office, the mechanical shops and the superintendent's house. The National Trust has a very difficult task trying to preserve the frail remnants that remain in the landscape today, but it is a task that many dedicated local people have been committed to for many years.

The National Trust Cottage at Moonta Mines is an example of a miner's home built in the early years of mining. It began as two rooms and, as the Cornish family grew, several additions were made to the original structure. All the rooms have now been tastefully restored and furnished in a style typical of a miner's home in the late nineteenth century. At Wallaroo Mines the house of the former captain of the Matta mine has been preserved and is also furnished in typical Cornish style. The house was originally built in 1863 and today is part of a large

The welcome sign to Australia's Little Cornwall on the roadside north of Moonta.

The National Trust miner's cottage at Moonta Mines.

Part of Wheal Munta, a National Trust reconstruction of mining machinery at Moonta Mines.

complex which includes an agricultural and printing museum.

In 1878, when Moonta Mines was booming, a large government school was built for hundreds of children who were being reared by the families on the mining leases. The school survived the cessation of mining, but eventually declining enrolments forced it to close in 1968. Now it is a National Trust museum and its large classrooms are filled with memorabilia of the Cornish mining days. It is visited by thousands of tourists every year; they come to recapture the Cousin Jack spirit that Moonta Mines had more than any other place in Australia. And just across the boundary fence of the schoolyard the National Trust has another project, its Wheal Munta mining display. Here the Trust has reconstructed some samples of machinery typical of the heyday of Moonta mining; a poppet head, a horse whim (a hoisting device operated by horse power), kibbles (egg-shaped buckets designed to convey ore in unlined shafts with a minimum of damage), and skips (rectangular iron boxes equipped with wheels which travelled up and down the shafts in guides).

The landscape of Australia's Little Cornwall contains two other features which have Cornish connections, Methodist churches and cemeteries. Only two of the fourteen original Methodist churches which were built at Moonta and Moonta Mines are being used today, one at Moonta and one at Moonta Mines. The Moonta Mines Uniting Church was built originally as a Wesleyan Church in 1865. It became the Moonta Mines Methodist Church in 1900 and the Moonta Mines Uniting Church in 1977. Still regularly used, it is nevertheless showing the effects of more than 100 years of continual use, and fears are held for its survival. The church accommodated up to 1200 devout Wesleyans at regular services in the 1870s through to the 1890s and many of their grandchildren of today are rallying to see that this historic landmark is not demolished in the same way as many of the small chapels of the district have been. Some still remain, not only at Moonta Mines, but in many other old mining communities throughout Australia. Characteristically they are small, box-like and unpretentious, but they remain as reminders of Cornish Methodist architecture which so often was deliberately designed to reflect a simple, uncomplicated faith, the antithesis of nineteenth-century high-church Anglicanism or Roman Catholicism.

The old mining communities also contain cemeteries, the headstones of which usually indicate the Trevorrows, Treloars, Polglases, Polkinghornes, Penglases, and so on, who were the early Cornish miners. None is more representative of the great Cornish migration than the Moonta cemetery where the names for any row read like an electoral roll for Cornwall. Wandering amongst the marble gravestones one encounters Methuselah Tregonning who died in 1876, Temperance Opie (died 1902), Josiah Perry (died 1943), Joshua Williams (died 1919), William Hercules Paynter (died 1931), Elijah Magor (died 1963) and numerous Trevithicks, Pascoes, Andrewarthas, Chappells, Martins, Rowes, Penaluricks, Pryors, Polkinghornes, Roddas, Penroses, Trembarths, Dunstans, Trewarthas, Penberthys, Trengroves and Tresizes.

Oswald Pryor claimed that in the nineteenth century amongst the world-wide mining fraternity there was a Cornish saying 'Has't ee been to Moonta? No? Then ees never travelled!' In the twentieth century the saying has relevance for thousands of descendants of the early Cornish miners. Moonta is part of their ancestral heritage and many of them make a pilgrimage to visit the home area of their grandparents.

What is there in Australian society today which can be traced back to the influence of the nineteenth-century Cornish? The most fundamental feature has already been mentioned many times, namely the surnames of the people. The Tre's, Pol's, Pen's and others are now widely spread throughout the continent. Thus a simple count through telephone directories for a very typical Cornish name like Polglase shows six in Brisbane, four in Perth, five in Hobart, thirteen in Sydney, fourteen in Adelaide and twenty-three in Melbourne. On a per capita basis this indicates a heavy concentration in Melbourne and Adelaide and this can undoubtedly be related to the fact that these two cities are the capitals of the two states in which most of the Cornish miners lived and worked.

Cornish Associations linger in Australian society today. They are groups of people who retain contacts with Cornwall, preserve a nostalgic interest in it as their 'homeland' and, increasingly, seek an awareness and appreciation of the heritage that the early Cornish brought to Australia. There is a Cornish Association of Sydney, a Loyal Devon, Cornwall and Somerset Association of Victoria, and a Cornish Association of South Australia. Of the three, the one that has been the most strongly supported this century has been the last mentioned.

Two influential and enthusiastic Cornishmen, James Penn Boucaut and John Langdon Bonython, founded the Cornish Association of South Australia at a banquet in the Adelaide Town Hall on 21 February 1890. The aims of the Association include 'to assist in forming and maintaining friendly intimacy and interest among those who are of Cornish birth or extraction' and 'to keep alive Cornish customs'. The first president was Boucaut; Bonython and W.B. Rounsevell were vice-presidents.

Branches of the Cornish Association of South Australia were started in Gawler, northern Yorke Peninsula, Kapunda and Clare. These country branches did not last long; they disbanded early in the 1900s as more and more of their district's old Cornish folk died or moved off to 'retire' in Adelaide. The parent body still meets regularly in Adelaide for 'Cornish Evenings' which usually begin with a pasty tea. Guest speakers, film evenings and carol singing evenings are typical features of an annual programme and, in recent years, special seminars have been conducted to concentrate on the Cornish heritage of the State. The association sells a range of Cornish books, magazines and selected souvenirs of Cornwall; it publishes a regular newsletter which gives news of Cornwall as well as items of social and local historical interest.

The Cornish love for singing their carols at Christmas time has been retained in South Australia in what is known as the Cornish Carol Choir. It began in Adelaide as the Moonta Harmony Choir in 1927 but in 1947 it adopted its present name. The choir performs regularly in the weeks before Christmas and an evening's entertainment is always given at Moonta.

Members of the choir are mostly descendants from the Cornish and they are representative of many thousands of people in Australia today who can trace their ancestry back to the miners who came from Cornwall. Unlike their ancestors, who were mostly poorly educated miners from the lower classes, many of the descendants have been in the forefront of Australian society. Sir Robert Menzies, Prime Minister of Australia, was the son of a Cornish miner's daughter who married James Menzies at Jeparit in Victoria. Robert Hawke, the present Prime Minister descends from Cornish copper miners at Kapunda. Field-Marshal Sir Thomas Blamey was the son of Richard Blamey, a Cornish immigrant of 1862. Geoffrey Blainey, the well-known Australian historian has a Cornish ancestry and so does Judith Wright the poet and David Tonkin the former Premier of South Australia.

In recent years there has been a great upsurge in family history studies and many Australians have discovered that their roots are with the Cornish. A Trevena family history and a Dunstan family history have highlighted early mining families in Kapunda and *The Days of May*, published in 1981, traces some 1365 descendants from Henry and Mary May who arrived in South Australia from Cornwall in 1858. When the book was launched in Gawler, the home of the old May engineering works, nearly 600 May descendants crowded on to Gawler's Pioneer Oval.

In addition to family histories highlighting our Cornish past, May Cocks, the secretary of the Cornish Association of South Australia for many years, has produced a booklet which publicises traditional Cornish cooking. Published in the Rigby's Instant book series, it gives recipes for such favoured Cornish delicacies as Leek pie, Treacle-tart, Fuggan, Saffron buns, Stargazy Pie and Figgy'obbin.

In 1973 the greatest revival of 'Cornishness' Australia has seen emerged in the form of the Kernewek Lowender which, loosely translated from the old Cornish language, means Cornish Festival. The Lowender was the brainchild of a group of business people in the towns of Moonta, Kadina and Wallaroo. They applied to the South Australian government for financial assistance and the Premier at that time, Don Dunstan, was enthusiastic. The government pledged support if the festival would stress the Cornish history of the district.

The first Lowender set a pattern that has been followed since. It was spread over a three-day long weekend in May and it was shared equally between the three towns. Kadina provided musical concerts led by the Kadina and Wallaroo Band (bandmaster Sam Trenwith) and supported by vocalists, the Cornish Carol Choir and the South Australian Folk Federation singing and playing Cornish folk songs. Wallaroo provided a Golya (Cornish Feast) in its Town Hall. A feature of the evening was the reintroduction of Swanky, a kind of home-brewed beer that had been unique to the Cornish of the area. The feast catered for 650 people and hundreds who did not book in advance had to be turned away. Moonta provided a Fer Kernewek (Cornish Fair) on its oval. The programme included Cornish wrestling, a pasty-making competition, a wheelbarrow race, a tug-of-war, and a competition for the best dressed Cousin Jack and Jenny. There was a festival procession to the oval and a traditional Cornish Furry Dance (Floral Dance).

The local organisers, who had formed themselves into Kernewek Lowender Incorporated, were astounded at the success of their venture. The festival takings exceeded $20 000, more than 12 000

Part of the crowd at the Kernewek Lowender in 1973 during the pasty-making competition. Don Dunstan, who was Premier of South Australia at the time, was taking part in the competition.

people attended the Fer Kernewek, more than 1000 dozen bottles of Swanky were sold out before the three days were over, the Moonta baker sold so many pasties on the Sunday that he didn't have enough flour for his orders on the Monday, and the petrol stations in Kadina sold out of super grade petrol on the Monday.

Since that first Kernewek Lowender there has been one held every May in the odd-numbered years, 1975, 1977, 1979 and 1981. In 1975 the *Yorke Peninsula Country Times* proclaimed the success of the three days in a headline 'Little Cornwall Pays a Divvy'. The article said:

> In the second Cornish Festival, Kadina, Wallaroo and Moonta on the weekend paid their biggest dividend since the copper mines closed in 1923. An estimate of the crowd watching the mile long procession through the streets of Moonta was 20 000 . . . More than a thousand worshippers packed the Moonta Mines Methodist Church for the Heritage Sunday Service.

The third Kernewek in 1977 was bigger again and in 1979 a record 25 000 people attended the Fer on the Monday.

There have now been five very successful Lowenders, and people of Cornish descent have come to recognise the event as the major gathering of their ethnic group in Australia. Many New Zealanders of Cornish extraction have also attended.

Kernewek Lowender Incorporated is still staffed by voluntary helpers in the district, but it is now able to employ a full-time co-ordinator to plan and assist with future festivals. The Lowenders have revived and perpetuated many aspects of Cornish life and, additionally, the famous Cornish folk-singer and story-teller Brenda Wootton was a guest artist in 1979 and 1981.

The aim of Kernewek Lowender Incorporated is 'to revive the traditions of the Cornish Heritage in the Northern Yorke Peninsula area and to co-ordinate all the functions of the Cornish Festival'. In achieving this aim on five occasions since 1973, the incorporated body has made it known to tens of thousands of Australians that the Cornish people who settled in our country during the nineteenth century were a colourful ethnic group who made a significant contribution to our economic development.